# MAKING
# SELF-TEACHING
# KITS FOR
# LIBRARY SKILLS

# MAKING SELF-TEACHING KITS FOR LIBRARY SKILLS

Marian E. Karpisek

AMERICAN LIBRARY ASSOCIATION
Chicago 1983

*Library of Congress Cataloging in Publication Data*

Karpisek, Marian E.
  Making self-teaching kits for library skills.

  1. School children—Library orientation—Handbooks,
manuals, etc.   I. Title.
Z711.2.K26   1983        025.5′678′222        82-18488
ISBN 0-8389-0374-6 (pbk.)

*To my husband, Bob,*
*and my daughters,*
*Kris and Jenny*

# CONTENTS

FIGURES     vii

ACKNOWLEDGMENTS     ix

## 1   INTRODUCTION     1

## 2   PARTS OF A BOOK     5

Materials Needed     5
Preparing the Script     5
Preparing the Follow-up Activity     5
Preparing for Student Use     6
Script     6
Follow-up Activity     9

## 3   CARD CATALOG     10

Materials Needed     10
Preparing the Visual Book     10
Preparing the Script     11
Preparing the Worksheet     11
Preparing for Student Use     11
Script     12
Worksheet     23

## 4   ENCYCLOPEDIAS     25

Materials Needed     25
Preparing the Visual Book     25
Preparing the Script     26
Preparing the Worksheet     26
Preparing for Student Use     26
Script     26
Worksheet     37

## 5 CHILDREN'S MAGAZINE GUIDE — 39

Materials Needed — 39
Preparing the Visual Book — 39
Preparing the Script — 40
Preparing the Worksheet — 40
Preparing for Student Use — 40
Script — 40
Worksheet — 49

## 6 ABRIDGED READERS' GUIDE TO PERIODICAL LITERATURE — 50

Materials Needed — 50
Preparing the Visual Book — 50
Preparing the Script — 51
Preparing the Worksheet — 51
Preparing for Student Use — 51
Script — 51
Worksheet — 63

## 7 ALMANACS — 64

Materials Needed — 64
Preparing the Visual Book — 64
Preparing the Script — 65
Preparing the Worksheet — 65
Preparing for Student Use — 65
Script — 65
Worksheet — 80

## 8 ATLASES — 81

Materials Needed — 81
Preparing the Visual Book — 81
Preparing the Script — 82
Preparing the Worksheet — 82
Preparing for Student Use — 82
Script — 82
Worksheet — 92

## 9 VERTICAL FILE — 93

Materials Needed — 93
Preparing the Sample File — 93
Preparing the Script — 93
Preparing for Student Use — 94
Script — 94
Follow-up Activity — 96

## CONCLUSION — 97

# FIGURES

Chapter 3: CARD CATALOG
FIG. 1. Author card — 13
2. Title card — 14
3. How title cards are filed — 14
4. Subject card — 15
5. Card for fiction — 15
6. Card for an easy book — 15
7. Card for story collection — 16
8. Card for nonfiction — 17
9. Card for biography — 18
10. Card for reference work — 18
11. Card for an audiovisual item — 19
12. "See" card — 20
13. "See also" card — 20
14. Dewey Decimal Classification — 20
15. How nonfiction books are shelved — 21
16. Shelf arrangement of nonfiction books with decimals — 21
17. Symbols and colors used to identify audiovisual materials — 22

Chapter 4: ENCYCLOPEDIAS
FIG. 18. Left-hand page of encyclopedia index with subject entry guide — 28
19. Right-hand page of encyclopedia index with subject entry guide — 29
20. Encyclopedia index entry — 30
21. Left-hand text page of encyclopedia — 31
22. Right-hand text page of encyclopedia — 32
23. Information elements in an encyclopedia entry — 33
24. Additional information elements — 34
25. Encyclopedia index main entry and subentries — 36

26. Index subentry picture reference — 35
27. Index entry for subject to be found under differing subject entries — 36

Chapter 5: CHILDREN'S MAGAZINE GUIDE
FIG. 28. Cover of September 1981 issue — 42
29. Abbreviations used for magazines indexed — 43
30. Index entry that shows abbreviated magazine title — 44
31. Another abbreviated magazine title — 44
32. Identifying the elements in an index entry — 45
33. Index entry with more than one reference — 46
34. Index entry with subheads that identify related subject entries — 46
35. Index "see" entry — 47
36. Index "see also" entry — 47
37. Sample page of index entries — 48

Chapter 6: ABRIDGED READERS' GUIDE TO PERIODICAL LITERATURE
Fig. 38. Cover of May 1981 issue — 53
39. Abbreviations for indexed publications — 54
40. Abbreviations for other words used in entries — 56
41. Identifying the elements of an index entry — 57
42. Elements of sample index entry — 59
43. Index entry with a subject heading and subhead — 60
44. Index "see" entry — 60
45. Index "see also" entry — 61

46. Index entry for book reviews          62

Chapter 7:  ALMANACS

Fig. 47. Index page                        66

48. Index entry—main subject heading
    with subheads                          67

49. Index entry for information to be
    found under differing subject
    headings                               68

50. Index entry with word in
    parenthesis                            68

51. Index entry with date in
    parenthesis                            68

52. Acronym in parenthesis following
    organization name in
    index entry                            68

53. Index "see" references                 69

54. Comparison of text page heading
    with index main entry                  71

55. Correlating text with first
    subentry                               72

56. Correlating text with second
    subentry                               73

57. Correlating text page information
    with third subentry                    74

58. Finding information on the
    almanac page                           75

59. Footnote reference in almanac
    entry                                  76

60. Where to look for information
    about a popular singer                 77

61. Entertainers, when and where they
    were born                              78

Chapter 8:  ATLASES

Fig. 62. Map of North America              83

63. Direction symbol                       84

64. Legend for the map of
    North America                          84

65. Sample scale of miles                  86

66. Determining distances on map
    of North America                       87

67. Gazetteer–Index                        89

68. Map of the western
    United States                          90

# ACKNOWLEDGMENTS

I am grateful to Paul E. Rafferty, Permissions Editor of *The World Book Encyclopedia*; Karen W. Richgruber, Editor of *Children's Magazine Guide*; Tom Fitzgerald, Director of Advertising for The H. W. Wilson Company; Jane D. Flatt, Vice President and Publisher of *The World Almanac*; and Betty Linberg of the Copyright Permissions Department of Hammond Incorporated for their assistance and encouragement. They were most cooperative in offering permission to use examples from their respective publications.

I also want to thank the Salt Lake City Board of Education and Superintendent M. Donald Thomas for their support of library programs. My experiences as a librarian with the Salt Lake City School District have given me the background I needed to write this manual.

This manual could not have been written without the support and encouragement of my husband.

# 1 INTRODUCTION

The happy sounds of children approaching filled the hall outside the library media center. Inside the door, however, I waited with trepidation. Usually, I looked forward to this time as much as the students did, but today I was going to begin teaching library skills. And from past experience I knew how the children were going to react.

I would use my best teaching manner and the finest audiovisual presentations available; but, if I were lucky, two or three children would leave at the end of the period with a good grasp of the skill I had presented. Not a very impressive success ratio, but how could I improve it?

As library media coordinators, we recognize the validity and necessity of teaching library skills to elementary school children. These are the age groups which *must* be taught to use reference materials if they are to succeed in school and develop lifelong learning skills. No one will dispute the value of teaching library skills; the problem lies in finding the best method to use.

Group orientation is the usual approach. A teacher brings a class to the library media center for the purpose of learning a specific skill. The children, however, are seldom receptive to what is being taught. Often there is a lack of interest because the need to put the information to work immediately is lacking. Even if the classroom teacher has cooperated by planning a project involving the skill, the motivation is seldom sufficient for everyone in the class.

There are some students who, because their minds wander off the task at hand, do not really hear what is presented. Other cannot relate what they have seen and heard to what they actually will

be doing. And, of course, there are always a few children who are absent on a given day; they miss the presentation entirely.

The best teaching moment occurs when the child is ready to learn and has a valid need to know. It is when a child wants to find a special book that card catalog skills become necessary, when he or she must do a map assignment that the time is right for teaching the use of atlases. Similarly, when finding information in an encyclopedia is required, the child will be receptive to learning to use an encyclopedia correctly.

In an ideal situation, a library media coordinator will be standing by, always on the alert for anyone needing assistance and ready to use the opportune moment to individually teach the requisite skill to each student. However, we all recognize that this is immensely impractical, if not implausible.

Commercially prepared materials are often entertaining and provide basic information, but they have one major deficit—they are produced by someone who has never been in your school and who has never experienced your unique situation. Therefore, the information they contain must be generalized and nonspecific. By creating your own kits for pupil self-instruction as described in this manual, you will make available information that is specific to your particular library. Also, by using examples from the actual resources to which the student has access, the instruction you are providing becomes valid in the eyes of the student. Furthermore, by interspersing comments which refer specifically to your own school, the student becomes aware of the relationship of the subject matter to reality.

# Kit Design

The kits to be produced by following this manual are designed to help you, the library media coordinator, teach library skills to students from grades three to six at the moment each child actually is ready to learn and in a way which will best help her or him to learn.

Children differ in their learning styles. Some learn best by reading, others by listening, and still others benefit most from a "hands-on" approach. The kits are designed to meet the needs of children who learn in all of these ways. In addition the kit is designed for self-teaching at a rate determined by the individual child.

*THE VISUAL BOOK.* The visual element is enhanced by the "visual book" which combines both print and nonprint information. Visual books accompany all kits except those for the parts of a book and the vertical file. The "Parts of a Book" kit relies on the book itself to provide the necessary visual information. The "Vertical File" kit uses a sample vertical file folder in place of the visual book.

*THE AUDIOTAPE.* The audio element is provided by the audiotape cassette which you will record using the script that is included in each chapter. Key words and phrases are reiterated in the script to reinforce the concepts in the child's mind. The cassette tape also provides a continuity between the visual book and the physical resource itself. It also provides the option of listening to the tape again to clarify concepts that were not understood. The student is able to stop the tape, reverse it, and listen to the audio message again and again.

*THE "HANDS-ON" COMPONENT.* The "hands-on" experience comes through use of the actual material resources available in your school. In the card catalog unit, the student uses your card catalog and the books actually on the shelves of your library media center. When learning to use the almanac, the child has an almanac from your collection at hand.

The kits take into consideration the fact that all children do not learn at the same rate. Each kit,

presented as a chapter in this manual, can be prepared either as a single module covering the complete teaching of one skill area, such as the card catalog, or as a set of separate modules that divide the skills into smaller units. If the kit is to be prepared as a single module, all of the material presented in the chapter will be put together as a continuous unit. The tape will include the entire script and the visual book will contain all the illustrations required to teach the specific skill.

If you feel that the children in your school will learn better if they are introduced to specific elements of a skill in smaller units, the kit can be broken into shorter modules by recording the script onto two or more audiotapes. A visual book containing illustrations for each section of script required by the unit must accompany each tape.

The card catalog unit, for example, could be prepared as four separate modules instead of one. The first module could cover the physical arrangement of the card catalog and the parts of a catalog card. The second module could include call numbers for fiction, easy, and story collection books. The section of script and the accompanying illustrations relating to the Dewey Decimal Classification System could become the third module. The final module could include biography, reference, audiovisual, and "See" and "See Also" cards.

Of course, two rather than four modules could contain all of the material or the script and visual material could be subdivided into even smaller components. As the designer of your individual kits, you decide upon the length of the modules; however, remember, each module must have its own audiotape and accompanying visual book.

Reinforcement or review is accomplished by referring to the visual book for specific information or by repeating the entire kit or module. This on-the-spot instruction and review is important because it assures the student access to the information at the precise moment it is needed.

# Content and Organization of *Manual*

This manual is designed to help you prepare individualized kits of library skills instruction for the students in your school. Each chapter includes complete and detailed instructions for making a specific kit.

First in each chapter is a brief overview of the skill to be taught with the kit presented in that chapter. This introduction validates the need for the kit and enumerates the behavioral objectives. Following this is a list of the software materials needed for producing that specific kit (colored pencils, blank cassette tape, felt-tip pen, and the like).

The next section gives complete directions for preparing the visual book. Each step is described in detail and, when applicable, you are referred to the corresponding illustration in this manual. The directions given (*see* fig. 7; 30) apply to the illustrations in this manual only. In making your visual books, you will refer to the illustrations as figure 1 or page 1, numbering each in succession, since each visual book is a complete entity in itself.

Step-by-step instructions are given for preparing the script for recording. The script itself follows the sections of text detailing those steps and contains the instructions needed to understand the use of any library and media center. As some libraries and school library media centers also share more distinctive characteristics in their organization, the manual includes so-labeled "options" for teaching the skills by taking into account these differences. The directions for the script instruct you to select the options which apply to your specific school. For example, in the kit for teaching the skill of using the card catalog, Option 2A will be used by a school which has a card catalog containing "See" and "See Also" cards. Option 2B will be used in a school that does not use "See" and "See Also" cards in the card catalog.

Each script also contains word options which are given in parentheses. An example from the script for the card catalog: "This is known as the (call/location/book) number...." You select the appropriate term you ordinarily use when speaking to students—call number, location number, or book number.

When a word refers specifically to the resource book being used, the term for the selected subject is given in parentheses. For example, in the almanac script, there is a sentence that reads: "(Oceans) will be found alphabetically in the (O) section after the letter (O)." If you have selected a different subject, you would instead substitute the word and appropriate opening letter of the subject of your choice. In addition, the script will often give you directions in italics. "The fiction books are (*describe the location*)." In your own words,

you will describe where the fiction books are located in your library media center.

Following the section of instructions for preparing the script, instructions for making the worksheet are detailed. A sample worksheet or follow-up activity follows the script in each chapter. These allow you to evaluate student application of the skill.

The last set of instructions helps you prepare for student use. This section is a checklist for ascertaining that the necessary hardware and software is assembled and ready for student use.

# Hardware and Software

You will need to have available for student use with each kit or separate module a battery-operated tape cassette player equipped with earphones. The number of cassette players may limit the number of modules you develop from any one kit. A minimum of one cassette player per kit module is essential. The number of modules per kit determines the number of players needed. For example, if the card catalog kit is prepared as four modules, four cassette players will be needed. In addition, you will need a tape recorder with a microphone for recording the scripts onto the cassette tapes. Access to a copy machine also is necessary to reproduce the illustrations in the visual book required for each kit.

Software items are minimal and those that are essential for producing a given kit are listed in the appropriate chapter. A complete list of software supplies required to complete all of the kits is given here for your convenience:

Blank audiocassette tapes (at least 8)
Colored pencils (9 colors)
Black felt-tip pen (1)
Two- or three-ring notebook binders (at least 6)
Mimeo or ditto masters (approximately 8)
Manila folder (1)
Catalog cards from the card catalog (*see* chapter 3)
Print resources (*see* individual kits)

# Kit Preparation

The first step in preparing the kits is to determine what reference sources you wish to use. The sources may be the same as those used in this manual provided you have these resource books available in your library media center. If you do not have the same titles used in this manual, you should select others from your collection.

When you have selected the requisite reference volumes, the illustrations for the visual book should be made. Again, you may elect to use the examples given in the manual or you may select others. That is, if you are using *The World Book Encyclopedia*, you may choose to use the examples given in this manual (tiger, circus, sunset) or you may choose other subjects in *The World Book Encyclopedia*. If you are using another encyclopedia, you will want to select subject illustrations that have details similar to those used in the examples.

After the visuals have been produced, the word choices for the script should be made. Circle the words and options you wish to include before you record your script. Write in the dialogue necessary to complete the script, such as your description of where your school library media center's books are located. This will make recording the script easier. Remember, the script must be coordinated with the visual book and the reference material at hand.

You may repeat sentences or words for emphasis and include additional script and illustrations for clarification. Do not hesitate to make any changes that will increase the relevancy of the material for your students.

At the beginning of each tape, you may wish to add the following information regarding the (*Tone*) sound:

> Whenever you hear this sound (*Tone*), stop the tape and do what the tape tells you to do. When you are ready to go on, start the tape again.

For a tone sound, you may want to use a xylophone, bell, or triangle. Whatever sound you favor, it is important that the tone remain constant throughout all of the tapes you make.

Finally, decide upon the desired length of the module and record the tape or tapes. When the tape is recorded and the accompanying visual book assembled, prepare an area where the kit can be set up in conjunction with the actual reference tool. When you have shown the students how to operate the tape cassette, they should be able to use the kits at their time of need with no further aid from you. You can proceed with classes and other tasks knowing that students are learning the skills in a meaningful way at the time when they have an expressed need to know.

# 2 PARTS OF A BOOK

For students to effectively utilize books, it is necessary that they understand the components of a book. This chapter introduces the student to the various parts of a book.

The student will learn to recognize and utilize a book's table of contents, bibliography, index, and glossary. In addition, the student will discover what information will be found on a book's title page, on the verso of the title page, on the book's cover or dust jacket, on its spine, and in its dedication. These elements are presented in terms that a second- or third-grade student can understand.

## Materials Needed:

1 Nonfiction book with the following features:
   a. Dust jacket (Option 1A)
   b. Half title page
   c. Dedication
   d. Table of contents
   e. Glossary
   f. Bibliography
   g. Index
                    or
Several nonfiction books incorporating several of the above features
1 Blank cassette tape.

## Preparing the Script:

1. Read the script and insert title, author, and other specific information.
2. Select terminology congruent with that used in your library media center.
3. Choose Option 1A or 1B, depending upon your use of dust jackets.
4. Choose Option 2A, 2B, or 2C.
5. Proofread the script to correct any oversights or errors.
6. Record the script onto the blank cassette tape.

## Preparing the Follow-up Activity:

1. This kit is designed to be used by students as young as second grade. Words which are associated with the parts of a book—i.e., glossary, dedication, bibliography, etc.—are words most children in the primary grades will not be able to read. To compensate for this, the follow-up

activity has been designed as an oral review. This can be done in three ways:

a. The questions are recorded and the student stops the tape after each one and answers silently or aloud. When the tape is started again, immediate feedback of the correct answer is received.

b. The library media coordinator and the student have a verbal interchange in which the questions are asked and answered.

c. The student is given instructions for recording the answers on another tape recorder equipped with a microphone. The student records the answers and the library media coordinator can listen at her or his convenience, checking the verbal answers.

2. Select a nonfiction book embodying the parts of a book included in the script.

3. Ask the questions used in the sample, eliminating any which cannot be answered by the book at hand.

# Preparing for Student Use:

1. Arrange a table and chair.
2. Put the recorded tape cassette into a cassette player with earphones.
3. If using Option 2C, set up an additional tape cassette recorder with a blank cassette tape and microphone.
4. Place a copy of the book (or books) to be used on the table.

# Script

You know what a book is. You have been reading books since you were in first grade, and you were looking at books before that. Today, you are going to learn about the parts of a book. I will be talking about the book titled (*give the title*), which is on the table in front of you.

*OPTION 1A: Dust jacket on book*

Pick up your book. This book is covered with a dust jacket. A dust jacket is put on a book for two reasons. One reason is that the dust jacket is more colorful than a plain book cover. The other reason why libraries use dust jackets is that they help keep the books clean. (To help keep the dust jackets in good condition, we also put a plastic cover over the dust jacket.)

The first thing you see when you pick up the book is the front of the dust jacket. On the front of the dust jacket, you see the name of the book (*enunciate the title of the book as it appears on the dust jacket*), and the name of the author (*give the author's name as it appears on the dust jacket*). You also see a picture on the front. The picture shows you something about the story. Its purpose is to make you want to read the book. This picture (*describe the picture*) makes you want to find out more about (*specify the subject*).

Turn the book over. (*Pause*) This is the back of the dust jacket. The back of the dust jacket (has a picture of the author [*give the author's name*]/tells about some of the other books [*author's name*] has written).

Under the dust jacket you will see the cover of the book; it is called the case. The sides of the case are called the boards. You will not see the boards themselves, because the outside surfaces are covered with cloth and the inside with paper. Buckram is one kind of cloth used for covering books.

Now place the book on the table so that it is facing you and standing up as it would be on the shelf in our (library/media center). (*Pause*) The narrow part of the case between the two boards is what you would see if you could see through the jacket. This is the spine of the book. The pages in the book are either sewn or glued together to make the spine. Your spine is made of bones and is a part of your skeleton that helps to hold you up; but the spine of a book holds its pages together. If you break your spine, you won't be able to walk; if a book's spine is broken, the book falls apart and can no longer be used.

The part of the dust jacket covering the spine tells you the title of the book (*give spine title*) and the author's (last) name (*give name as it appears on the spine*). It also tells you the name of the publisher (*give publisher's name as it appears on the spine*). This information is on the spine to help you find the book easily when it is on the shelf.

Open the front cover of your book. (*Pause*) The inside flap of the front dust jacket tells you a little about the story or subject found in the book. It is written so that you will want to read the entire book. This is called a "teaser" or "blurb."

Turn to the inside of the back cover. (*Pause*) The inside flap of the back of the dust jacket (tells you about the author [*give author's name*]/ tells you about other books the author [*give author's name*] has written/completes the blurb begun on the front of the dust jacket).

*OPTION 1B: No dust jacket*

The cover of the book in front of you is called the case. The sides of the case are called the boards. You cannot see the boards because their outside surfaces are covered with cloth and the inside surfaces are covered with paper. Pick up the book and turn it so that it is facing you as it would be on the shelf in our (library/media center). The narrow part of the case that you see between the two boards is the spine of the book. The pages of the book are either sewn or glued together to make its spine. Your spine is made of bones and is the part of your skeleton that helps to hold you upright; but the spine of a book is what holds its pages together. If you were to break your spine, you would be unable to walk; if a book's spine is broken, the book falls apart and can no longer be used.

There is no printing on either the front or back of the case of this book. The spine is where you will find its title (*give title as it appears on the spine*) and the author's (last) name (*give name as it appears on the spine*). It also tells you the name of the publisher (*give publisher's name as it appears on the spine*). All this information is on the spine to help you find the book easily when it is on the shelf.

[End of Option 1]

Open the front of your book to the page that has *only* the title on it. It will be (*give number of pages from cover*) pages from the cover. (*Pause*) The page that reads (*give the title as it appears on the half title page*) is called the half title page. It is called the half title page because it only has about half of the information that is given on the title page.

Turn the page. (*Pause*) This is the title page of the book. This page tells you the author's name (*give the author's name as it appears on the title*

*page*), and the full title of the book (*give the title as it appears on the title page*).

At the bottom of the title page is the name of the company that published the book. The publisher is the company that selects, edits, designs, prints, and sells the book. Sometimes it pays people outside the company to do some of these jobs. The publisher of (*give the title again*) is (*the name of the publishing company*). Under the name of the publishing company is the city where the publishing company is located. (*Name of publishing company*) is in (*give city [and state]*).

Turn the title page over. (*Pause*) The back of the title page tells you when the book was copyrighted. The copyright sign is a small letter "c" inside a circle. Copyright tells you that no one can copy more than a few lines from the book without getting written permission from the publisher. The year of the copyright is the year in which the book was printed. (*Name of book*) was copyrighted and printed in (*give year*).

The country where the book was printed may also be given on this page. (*Name of book*) was printed in (the United States of America). Do you see where this is written on the page? (*Pause*)

The page facing the copyright page is the dedication page. Most authors give special credit to someone whom they especially wish to honor. (*Name of author*) dedicated (*name of book*) to (*rephrase the dedication to specify the receivers of the dedication*). The dedication of this book reads (*read the dedication*).

Turn to (*page with the table of contents*). (*Pause*) This is the table of contents page. The table of contents lists each chapter and the page on which it begins. Chapter 1 is (*give chapter title*) and it begins on page (*specify*). (*Give title of chapter 2*) is the second chapter and it begins on page (*specify*).

What is the title of chapter 4? (*Pause*) (*Give title of chapter 4*) is the title of chapter 4. On what page does chapter 6 begin? (*Pause*) If you said that chapter 6 begins on page (*specify*), you are doing very well!

Turn to page (*give page number where chapter 1 begins*). Here you see the title of chapter one (*give the title of chapter 1*). This is where the contents of the book begin. The contents of the chapters are called the text. The biggest part of any book is the text, which begins with chapter 1.

Now, turn to the back of the book, past the

text. Find page (*specify first glossary page*) at the back of (*title of book*). That's page (*repeat page number*). (*Pause*) This is the section of the book that is called the glossary. The glossary is a small dictionary of special words used in this book (*give the title of the book*). The glossary of this book includes words (*tell what kind of words are included in the glossary*). (*Sample glossary word*) means (*read definition*).

The words in the glossary are in alphabetical order, just as they would be in a dictionary. Can you find (*choose a word from the glossary*)? That's spelled (*spell the word*). (*Pause*) Did you find that the meaning of (*glossary word*) is (*read definition*)? Keep up the good work!

Let's go on to page (*specify first page of bibliography*). That is page (*repeat page number*). (*Pause*) This is the bibliography. The bibliography is a list of other books in which you can find more information on the subject the author(s) wrote about in this book. The bibliography of (*give title of book*) has a list of books which will give you more information about (*specify subject of book*).

(*Read the first bibliographic entry.*) This is a book that you might read to find more information about (*name of subject*). We (*do not*) have this book in our (*library/media center*).

You are ready to go to the index. Turn to page (*specify page on which index begins*). That's page (*repeat page number*). (*Pause*) The index is a list of subjects that you can read about in this book. It tells you the exact page(s) on which you will find a specific subject in the book. The index is in alphabetical order. Let's look at the first subject in the index. The first subject listed in the index is (*name*). You can find information about (*specify*) on page(s) (*give page or page numbers*).

(*Choose a fairly easy index entry*) is another subject listed in the index. Can you find what page in your book will have information on (*specify index entry*)? (*Pause*) If you discovered that information about (*index subject*) is on page (*specify*), you are using the index correctly.

Now find page (*specify text page just mentioned*) in the book and look at the information on (*index subject*). That's page (*specify*). (*Tone*)

By now you should be able to find all parts of any book. Remember, the table of contents is in the front. The glossary, the bibliography, and the index are in the back.

*OPTION 2A: Student response with taped feedback*

Let's see if you can answer some questions about the parts of a book. You will need to answer each question and then check your answer with the answer given on the tape. If you haven't given the right answer, stop the tape and see if you can find the answer that was given on the tape. The book you will use is located (*describe where you have placed this book*). (*Tone*)

*OPTION 2B: Dialogue between library media coordinator and student*

When you feel that you know the parts of a book, see me and we will talk about what you have learned.

*OPTION 2C: Student taping answers*

You are going to record your answers to some questions onto a tape. Listen to the questions on the tape you have been using. Then stop that tape, find the answer to the question, and record your answer into the microphone of the other cassette. To record (*give description of how to start and stop the recording process. Repeat these instructions for clarification*).

[End of script]

## FOLLOW-UP ACTIVITY

Questions to be used with Options 2A and 2C.  (Option 2C only:  Record your name onto the tape.)  (Tone)

1.  What is the title of this book?  (Tone)

2.  Who is the author of this book?  (Tone)

3.  Who published this book?  (Tone)

4.  What is the copyright date of this book?  (Tone)

5.  To whom did the author dedicate this book?  (Tone)

6.  Is the table of contents in the front or back of this book?  (Tone)

7.  What is the title of chapter 1?  (Tone)

8.  On what page does chapter 3 begin?  (Tone)

9.  Is the glossary in the front or back of the book?  (Tone)

10.  Is the index in the front or back of the book?  (Tone)

11.  What is the bibliography?  (Tone)

(If your answers to these questions were wrong, rewind the tape and listen again to the first part that told you about the parts of a book. [To be used if Option 2A is selected.])

# 3 CARD CATALOG

The ability to locate print and nonprint materials via the card catalog is essential if a student is to effectively utilize your library media center and other libraries. This kit introduces the student to the function and use of the card catalog.

The student will discover the physical arrangement of the catalog and will learn to use the three basic types of cards: author, title, and subject. The student will learn to decode call numbers and will learn where easy, fiction, story collection, nonfiction, biography, and reference books are located in your library media center.

The student will be introduced to the ten major classifications of the Dewey Decimal Classification System and will learn how nonfiction books are arranged by their Dewey Decimal Classification System numbers. The student will learn to locate nonprint media through the card catalog and will learn to locate subjects through "See" and "See Also" cards or by using related words.

The student will apply the concepts taught in this kit by finding designated cards in the card catalog and locating specific books in your library media center.

## Materials Needed:

Cards from your card catalog (see "Preparing the Visual Book")

3 Colored pencils (blue, yellow, and green)
1 Felt-tip pen (black)
1 Two- or three-ring notebook binder
1 Blank cassette tape
2 Mimeo or ditto masters.

## Preparing the Visual Book:

1. Pull the following cards from your card catalog:
   a. Fiction book: author, title, and subject cards
   b. Book with a title beginning with article "The": title card
   c. Easy book: title card
   d. Story collection book: author card
   e. Nonfiction book: subject card
   f. Biography: author card
   g. Reference book: main entry card
   h. Filmstrip: main entry card (Option 1)
   i. "See" and "See also" cards (Option 2A).
2. Use a copy machine to transfer each card to standard 8½" x 11" paper (see fig. 1).
   a. With a black felt-tip pen, draw a line around a card centered horizontally on an 8½" x 11" sheet of paper.
   b. Use the black lines as a guide for centering each card. Masking tape will hold the card in place while photocopying.

c.  Make one copy of each card. Exception: make 2 copies of the author card for the fiction book.
3.  Label the parts of the cards using a black felt-tip pen (*see* figs. 1–13).
4.  Use the colored pencils to identify parts of the author, title, and subject cards:
    a.  Color the author's name blue on the author card (fig. 1).
    b.  Color the title yellow on the title card. Both title lines should be colored (*see* fig. 2).
    c.  Color the subject heading green on the subject card (*see* fig. 4).
5.  Type or write the 10 main classes of the Dewey Decimal Classification System (*see* fig. 14).
6.  Type or write examples of Dewey Decimal call numbers (*see* figs. 15 and 16).
7.  Type or write a list of your audiovisual symbols if using Option 1 (*see* fig. 17).
8.  Make copies, if desired, for replacement purposes.
9.  Laminate the pages or insert into plastic protective sheaths for durability.
10. Punch two or three holes in the top (11″ side) of each page.
11. Put into notebook binder in the following order:
    a.  Author card
    b.  Title card
    c.  Title card for title beginning with "The"
    d.  Subject card
    e.  Fiction card
    f.  Easy fiction card
    g.  Story collection card
    h.  Dewey Decimal Classification System
    i.  Nonfiction book arrangement
    j.  Nonfiction book arrangement with decimals
    k.  Nonfiction card
    l.  Biography card
    m.  Reference card
    n.  Audiovisual card
    o.  Audiovisual symbols card
    p.  "See" card
    q.  "See also" card.

# Preparing the Script:

1.  Read the script and select and/or substitute the terminology congruent with that used in your library/media center.
2.  Decide which options to include.
3.  Insert your titles and the accompanying information into the script.
4.  Proofread the script to correct any oversights or errors.
5.  Record the script onto the blank cassette tape.

# Preparing the Worksheet:

1.  Type the worksheet exactly as it is written
    
    or
2.  Substitute other examples for those given.
3.  To make the card for question 1:
    a.  Trace the outline of a catalog card
    b.  Type in the information.

# Preparing for Student Use:

1.  Place an armchair desk close to the card catalog.
2.  Insert the recorded cassette tape into a battery-powered cassette player with headphones. Place the cassette player on top of the card catalog, if possible. It also may be placed on the arm of the armchair desk or on a small table set near the card catalog.
3.  Give the student the visual book.

# Script

You are sitting in front of our card catalog. The cards inside this catalog can help you find books and information. There are cards for the author, title, and subject of each book found in the (*name of your school library/media center*).

First, let's look at the card catalog itself. Notice that each drawer of the card catalog is labeled with (a letter/letters) of the alphabet. Open a drawer. All of the cards in this drawer are in alphabetical order by the first word on the card.

When you hear this sound (*Tone*), stop the tape and take a few minutes to look through several drawers to see how the cards are arranged. Whenever you hear this sound, stop the tape until you have completed the directions. You may also stop the tape whenever you need or want more time. Now, stop and see in what order the cards are arranged in the card catalog. (*Tone*)

A catalog card can tell you many things. Let's begin by discovering what you can learn when you look at one of these cards. We will start with an author card. Open your booklet to page 1 (*see fig. 1*) and look at the sample card. Here you see that the first word on the catalog card is the author's last name. You will find this card in the drawer which contains the (Os). The author's last name is always written first, followed by the author's first name. This author's name is (Mary O'Hara) and, on the card, it is written (O'Hara, Mary). The author's name is colored blue on page 1 to help you find it. Under the author's name is the title of the book, (*My friend Flicka*). Following the title of the book is the name of the person who drew the pictures for the book, the illustrator whose name is (*Dave Blossum*). Next, you can see the name of the company which published the book and the date the book was published. It was published by (Lippincott) in (1969). On the next line, you can find how many pages the book has and whether the book is illustrated. (*My friend Flicka*) has (266) pages and is illustrated.

Go to our book shelves and choose a book. Then look in the card catalog and find the author

card. (*Tone*) Did you find the author card for your book? Compare the information on the card with the book itself. Can you tell how many pages the book has? What company published this book? (*Pause*) When was it published? (*Pause*) Is it illustrated? (*Pause*)

Turn to page 2 (fig. 2) in your booklet. This page shows a title card. The title of the book has been colored yellow on this sample page. This card is filed in the (M) drawer. Why? (*Pause*) (My) is the first word of the title, (*My friend Flicka*), which makes (My) the first word on the title card and (My) begins with (M). Look at the cards on pages 1 and 2. Do you see that they are exactly alike, except that on the title card the title is printed twice, once under the author's name and once above the author's name? The title card gives you exactly the same information that the author card does, but it helps you find a book if you only know the title. To find a book when you know the title, look for the first word of the title.

Turn to page 3 (fig. 3). The only exception to finding books by the first word of the title is when the first word of the title is "A," "An," or "The." So many titles begin with these words that the words "A," "An," and "The" are omitted (or ignored) when the card is being filed alphabetically. Instead, the title is alphabetized under the second word. An example is the book called (*The great McGoniggle's gray ghost*). This title would be found in the (G) drawer for (Great), not in the (T) drawer for The. Can you locate this catalog card in our card catalog? (*Tone*)

You will also want to use the card catalog to help you find books when you are interested in a certain subject but do not know the titles of any books on that subject or any authors who have written about that subject. To find books this way, you will look for a subject card.

An example of a subject card is shown on page 4 (fig. 4). (*Pause*) Again, notice that this card is exactly like the author card except this time the subject is printed in capital letters above the author's name. The subject heading, (HORSES—FICTION), is colored green on the sample card. The subject heading is always written in capital letters and appears above the author's name. This subject card would be found in the (H) drawer. Why? (*Pause*) Right! It will be in the (H) drawer because (HORSES) begins with an (H).

Now you know how to find a card for a book in

# AUTHOR CARD

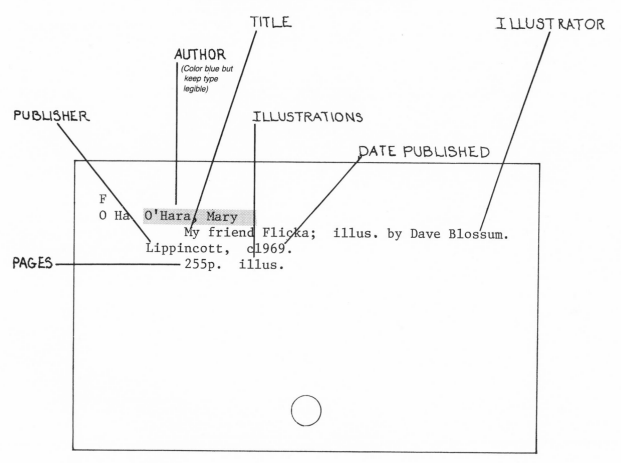

FIG. 1.   Author card

the card catalog by using an author's name, a title, or a subject, but how can you find the book you want on the shelves? Turn to page 5 (fig. 5). (*Pause*)

This card is the same card you have been looking at, but now notice the left-hand side of the card. There is a black line drawn around some letters (and numbers). This is known as the (call/location/book) number and it is what will help you find this book on our shelves. The (F) means that this book is fiction and it will be located in the fiction section of our (library/ media center). Fiction means that the story is made up and not real. The (letters/letter and numbers) below the (F) are symbols for the author's last name. Fiction books are arranged

alphabetically on the shelves by the authors' last names. Take a look at our fiction books and notice how they are in order by the authors' last names. The fiction books are (*describe the location*). (*Tone*)

We have another type of fiction book in our (library/media center). On page 6 (fig. 6), you will find a card for a book you may have read when you were just beginning to read. Look at the (call/location/book) number in the black box. This (call/location/book) number has (an E) and under that, a (V). The (E) stands for (Easy) and the (V/Vio) stands for the author's last name (Viorst). Cards with this type of (call/ location/book) number can be found (*describe the location*). No matter how old you are, it is fun to look at these books. Do you remember an old favorite of yours? Find the title in the card catalog and then see how much easier it is to find the book now that you know how to use the (call/location/book) number. (*Tone*)

The card on page 7 (fig. 7) is for a book which has a collection of short stories. The letters (SC/SS) stand for (Story Collection/Short Stories). Again, the (letters/letter and numbers) under the (SC/SS) stand for the author's last name. You will find (story collections/short stories) together in our (library/media center). They are found (*describe the location*). They, too, are in order by the authors' last names. If you have never looked for (story collections/short stories), stop the tape and see if you can locate them. (*Tone*)

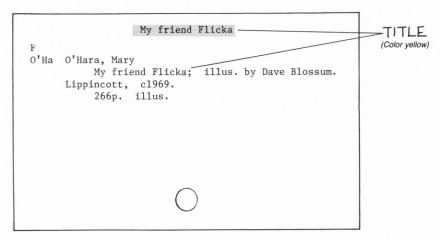

FIG.  2.   Title card

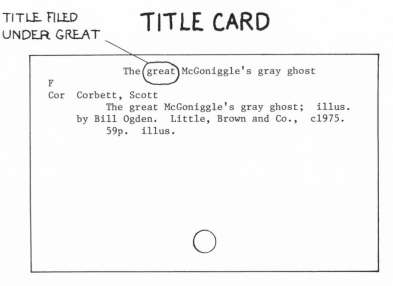

FIG.  3.   How title cards are filed

## SUBJECT CARD

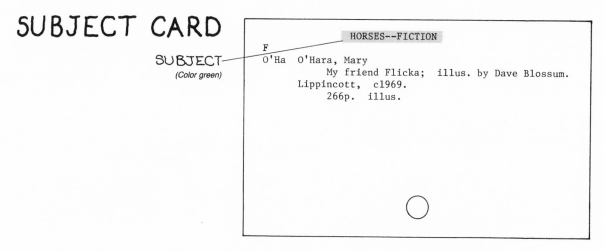

SUBJECT
*(Color green)*

HORSES--FICTION

```
F
O'Ha   O'Hara, Mary
            My friend Flicka;   illus. by Dave Blossum.
       Lippincott,  c1969.
            266p.  illus.
```

FIG. 4. Subject card

## FICTION CARD

CALL NUMBER

FICTION
AUTHOR

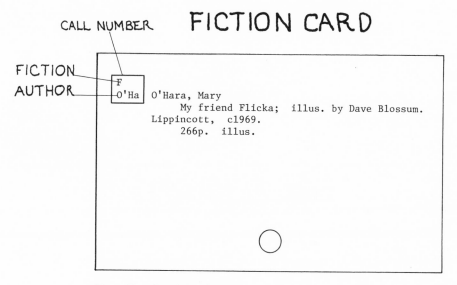

```
F
O'Ha   O'Hara, Mary
            My friend Flicka;   illus. by Dave Blossum.
       Lippincott,  c1969.
            266p.  illus.
```

FIG. 5. Card for fiction

## EASY BOOK

CALL NUMBER
EASY
AUTHOR

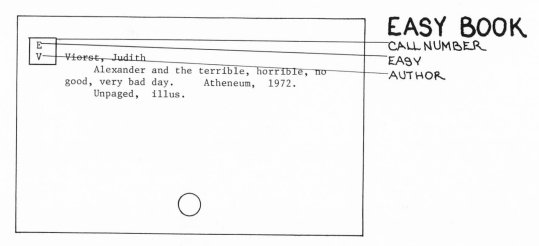

```
E
V   Viorst, Judith
        Alexander and the terrible, horrible, no
    good, very bad day.        Atheneum,  1972.
        Unpaged,  illus.
```

FIG. 6. Card for an easy book

# STORY COLLECTION CARD

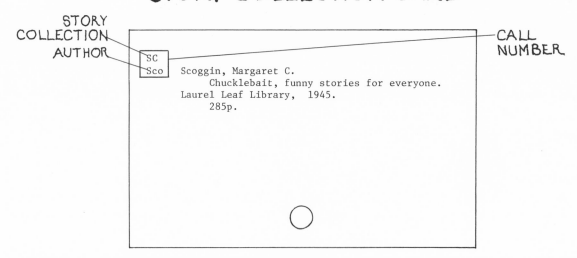

FIG. 7.　Card for story collection

Turn to page 8 (fig. 14). (*Pause*) Nonfiction books contain true facts and information and make up the largest part of the collection in most (libraries/media centers). Nonfiction books are located on the shelves by their Dewey Decimal Classification numbers.

Melvil Dewey was the man who created this method of numbering books. He felt that it would be easier to find nonfiction books if all books on the same subject were grouped together in one place. Dewey selected general headings and gave them numbers, such as 100, 200, 300, and so on. He then divided these headings until each subject had its own number. Here, on page 8, are the general topics of the Dewey Decimal numbers. I will read a sample of the material that you can find in each category.

The zeros include all numbers from 001 to 099.99 and the heading is "Generalities." Not too many of our books fall into this category, but some that do are encyclopedias and dictionaries.

The one hundreds are made up of the numbers from 100 to 199.99. These are books about philosophy, psychology, and other similar subjects. In the 100s, we have books about witches, ghosts, and feelings.

The two hundreds contain books about religion in general and specific religions such as Christianity, Judaism, and Hinduism. Books of myths also are found in this section.

The three hundreds cover topics in the so-cial sciences, such as politics, crime, government, education, transportation, folklore, and fairy tales.

The four hundreds are books that tell about language. Books about the English language and how to use it are shelved here. Stories written in other languages, such as Spanish and French, (are in this area also/can be found in the 400s in some libraries, but not in our library/media center).

Books about the pure sciences are placed in the five hundreds. The 500s include books with information on math, birds, animals, trees, flowers, and dinosaurs.

The six hundreds are books with the theme of technology. If you are interested in medicine, radios, ships, cars, farming, cooking, sewing, printing, or woodworking, you will look in the six hundred section.

Books about the arts are found in the seven hundreds. The 700s deal with many forms of art including photography, drawing, music, painting, and dancing. All books about sports, such as (*name any sports books which are popular in your library/media center*) are located in the seven hundreds.

The eight hundreds are books of literature. It is in this section that you will find poetry, speeches, and plays.

General geography and history are the main subjects found in the nine hundreds. Here you can locate books about the geography or history of all the countries of the world. Books about (*your state*) are in this section.

Now that you have a general idea of the Dewey Decimal Classification System, you are ready to learn how to find nonfiction books on the shelves of our (library/media center) by using the Dewey Decimal numbers.

Turn to page 9 (fig. 15). Nonfiction books are arranged on the shelves in the order of their Dewey Decimal numbers. The smallest numbers come first, followed by larger ones. Here book numbers are shown as they would be in order by their Dewey Decimal numbers. Only when two books have the exact same number is the author's name also used to find the book. Notice that (616 Dew) comes before (616 Kri). (*Pause*)

On page 10 (fig. 16) some more numbers are arranged as books would be placed on the shelves. (*Pause*) Notice that a book number without a decimal point comes before the same number followed by a decimal point. 973 comes before 973.71. It may help you to think of the numbers in terms of money. Do you have more money if you have (973) dollars or (973) dollars and (71) cents? (*Pause*) Think of the number past the decimal point as adding more to the number, making that number larger. Therefore,

(973.71) is larger the (973) because it has a point (seventy one) added to it.

Now look at the numbers (973.71 and 973.8). The number (973.71) is smaller than (973.8). The first number to the right of the decimal is the one to look at first. (973.7) is smaller than (973.8). All numbers that begin with (973.7) will be smaller than those beginning with (973.8). (973.71) is smaller than (973.8) and (973.79) would also be smaller than (973.8) because (7) is always less than (8).

Now spend a few minutes looking at the nonfiction books in our (library/media center). They are located (*describe the location*). See how these books are arranged by their Dewey Decimal numbers. (*Tone*)

Do you understand how books are placed in order according to their Dewey Decimal numbers? (*Pause*) Then you are ready for page 11 (fig. 8). This is a catalog card for a nonfiction book. The black box again marks the (call/location/book) number. In this case, the Dewey Decimal number is (641.5) and the subject is (COOKERY). This means that not only will you find the book (*Kids cooking; a first cookbook for children*) in the (641.5) area, but also all the books about (cooking) that we have at (*name of school*).

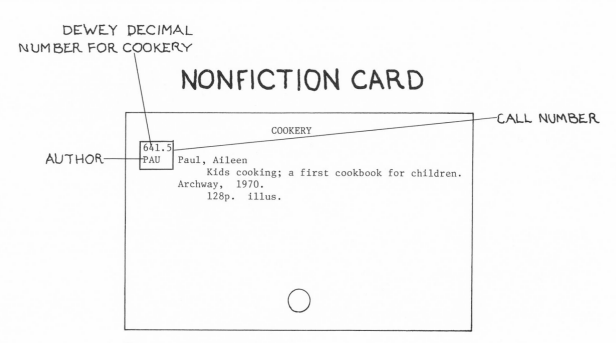

FIG. 8. Card for nonfiction

Turn to page 12 (fig. 9). Biographies are stories about real people and they are shelved together in one place. These books are labeled (B for Biography/92/921 for the Dewey Decimal number). Notice that the (letters/letter and numbers) under the (B/92/921) do not stand for the author's name, but for the person about whom the book was written. The author's name is printed in the usual place on the card, but the subject's name is used in the (call/location/ book) number. This is done so that all books about one person will be together on the shelves. Look in the card catalog for Abraham Lincoln. Remember to look in the Ls for Lincoln, not in the As for Abraham. Last names are always written first for authors and for subjects.

How many biographies of Abraham Lincoln do we have? (*Tone*) Did you notice that Lincoln's name was used in the (call/location/book) number rather than the author's name?

Now look at page 13 (fig. 10). (*Pause*) (R/Ref) above the (call/location/book) number means that the book you are interested in is a reference book. The Dewey Decimal number is the number for the subject, as usual, but the (R/Ref) means that the book will not be in the regular collection, but in the reference collection. Our reference books are located (*describe the location*). Reference books include encyclopedias, dictionaries, atlases, (*name any others you wish to include*).

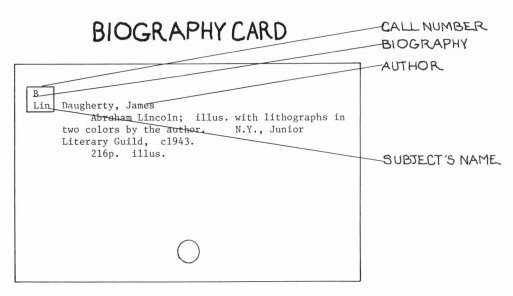

FIG. 9.   Card for biography

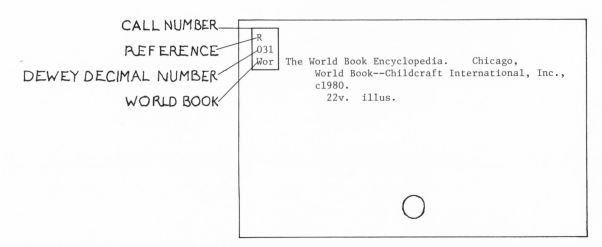

FIG. 10.   Card for reference work

*OPTION 1A: Audiovisual by Dewey Decimal
Number*

The card catalog also has cards for all the audiovisual materials in our (library/media center). Page 14 (fig. 11) shows a catalog card for a filmstrip. (*Pause*) The (call/location) number tells you where this filmstrip will be found in our (library/media center). (962) is the Dewey Decimal number for (Egypt) and, since this filmstrip is about (Egypt), you will find this filmstrip with all of our (materials/audiovisual materials) on (Egypt).

The (word, Filmstrip/symbol, FS) tells you that this is a filmstrip. (To help you identify audiovisual materials more easily, we give each type of audiovisual item a color code. This is a colored line that goes across the top of every audiovisual card.)

Page 15 (fig. 17) shows you the different symbols (and colors) we use for audiovisual materials. (*Pause*) (*Read your list.*) Our audiovisual materials are found (on the shelves with books about the same subject/in a special area of our library/media center—*describe*). You may use them by (*explain the process*).

*OPTION 1B: Audiovisual by accession number*

The card catalog also has cards for all the audiovisual materials in our (library/media center). Page 14 shows a catalog card for a filmstrip.

The (call/location) number tells you that the card you are looking at is for a filmstrip. The (word, Filmstrip/symbol, FS) tells you that this

is a filmstrip. The number (11) is the number for the filmstrip, ("Egypt, land of the Nile"). (*Describe your system of accession numbers.*) (To help you identify audiovisual material more easily, we give each type of audiovisual item a color code. This is a colored line which goes across the top of every audiovisual card.)

Look at page 15. This page shows you all of the symbols (and colors) for audiovisual materials. (*Read the list.*) Our audiovisual materials are found (*describe the location*). You may use them by (*explain the process*).

[End of Option 1]

*OPTION 2A: "See" and "See also" cards*

There are two other kinds of cards that you will find in our card catalog. Page (14/16) (fig. 12) shows a "See" card. This card tells you that although there are no books listed with the subject heading you have chosen, if you will look for the "See" subject, you will find the material you are hunting. For example, there is no subject heading (CARS). Instead, you should look for the subject (AUTOMOBILES).

Page (15/17) (fig. 13) shows a "See also" card. This card tells you that although you will find information with the subject heading you chose, you will find more information in other places. For instance, if you look for the subject (POLICE), you will find that we have some material with this subject heading. However, you will find additional material if you also look for the subjects (CRIME and DETECTIVES).

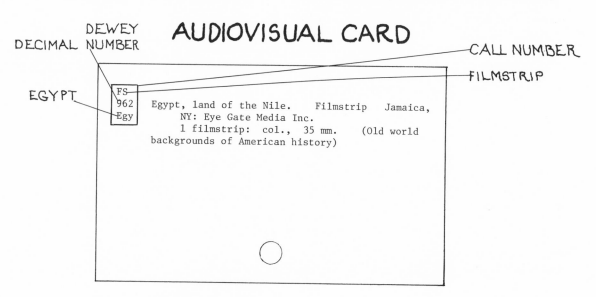

FIG. 11.   Card for an audiovisual item

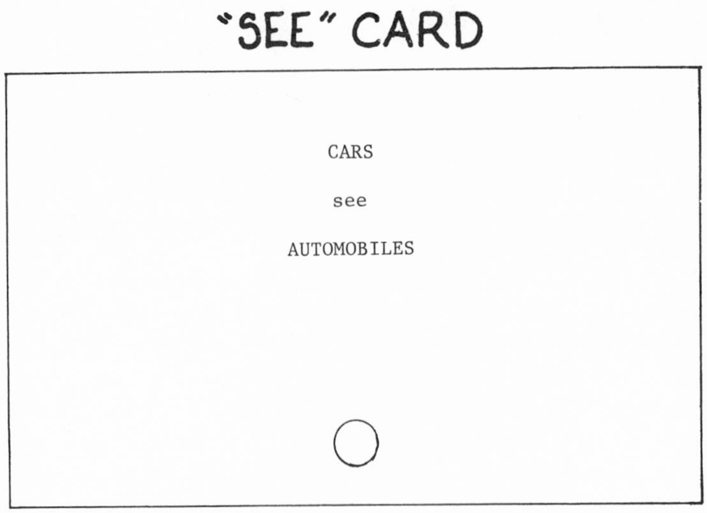

# "SEE" CARD

CARS

see

AUTOMOBILES

FIG. 12.   "See" card

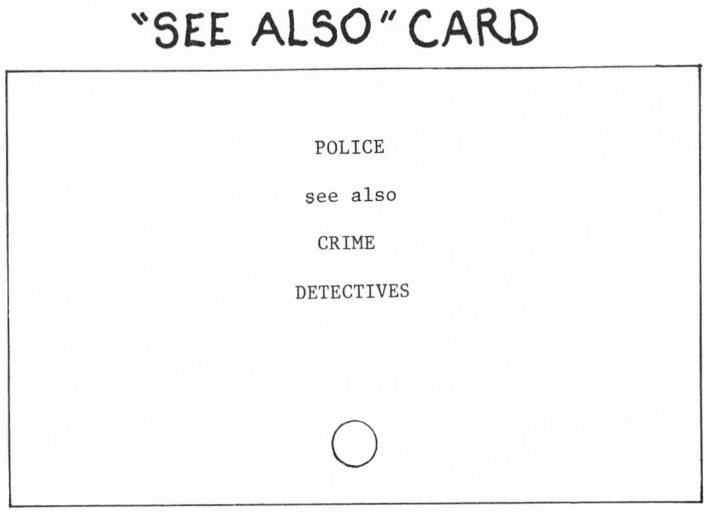

# "SEE ALSO" CARD

POLICE

see also

CRIME

DETECTIVES

FIG. 13.   "See also" card

DEWEY DECIMAL CLASSIFICATION

The 10 Main Classes

| | |
|---|---|
| 000 | Generalities |
| 100 | Philosophy and related disciplines |
| 200 | Religion |
| 300 | Social sciences |
| 400 | Language |
| 500 | Pure sciences |
| 600 | Technology (Applied Science) |
| 700 | The arts |
| 800 | Literature |
| 900 | General geography and history |

FIG. 14.   Dewey Decimal Classification

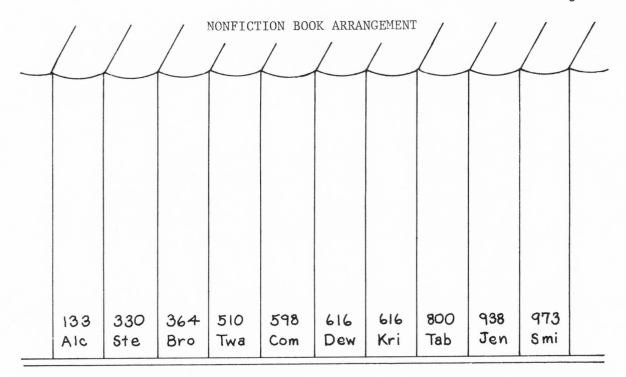

Fig. 15. How nonfiction books are shelved

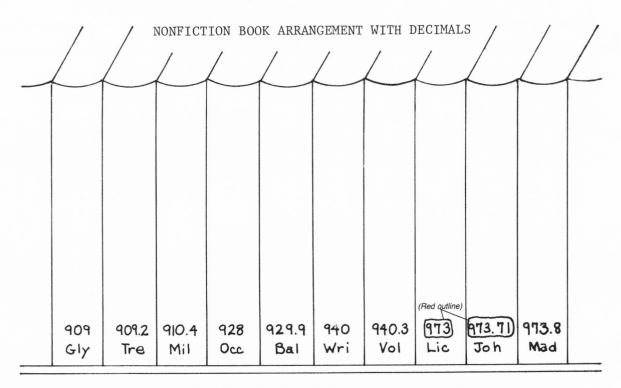

Fig. 16. Shelf arrangement of nonfiction books with decimals

AUDIOVISUAL MATERIALS

| | Symbol | Color |
|---|---|---|
| Audio Recordings | | |
| Phonograph records | RD | green |
| Tapes--Reel | RT | orange |
| Tapes--Cassette | RTC | orange |
| | | |
| Dimensional Materials | | |
| Models and Mockups | MOD | purple |
| Realia | R | purple |
| Maps | MAP | purple |
| | | |
| Flat Materials | | |
| Pictures | P | blue |
| Charts & graphs | C | blue |
| | | |
| Kits | | |
| Multimedia | KM | purple |
| | | |
| Transparent Materials | | |
| Microfilm | MF | red |
| Microfiche | MFC | red |
| Filmstrips | FS | red |
| Slides (2 X 2) | S | red |
| Transparencies | TR | brown |
| | | |
| Videotape | VT | yellow |

FIG. 17.   Symbols and colors used to identify audiovisual materials
Courtesy of the Utah State Office of Education.

*OPTION 2B: Card catalog without "See" and "See also" cards*

Sometimes you may look for a subject and not find it in the card catalog. Try to think of another subject heading which means about the same thing. For example, if you want to find a book about (CARS), you will not find this subject in our card catalog although we do have books about (CARS). Another word for (car) is (automobile) and if you will look for the subject heading (AUTOMOBILES), you will find the information you want.

[End of Option 2]

By now you should understand the way our card catalog is arranged and how it can help you locate books (and audiovisual materials). Spend some time looking in the card catalog for authors, titles, or subjects that you are interested in and then see if you can locate some of the books on the shelves without any help. If you do not remember something, play through the tape again or look at the visual book. If you still need help, ask (*your name*). When you are sure that you understand the material, complete the worksheet which (*your name*) will give you. You should be able to find the answers in the card catalog. Good luck!

[End of Script]

*WORKSHEET*

1.

```
                        DOLLS
   745.59
   Wen     Wendorff, Ruth
                How to make cornhusk dolls.    Arco, 1973.
                77p.  illus.




                          ◯
```

    a.    The author of this book is _____

    b.    The title of this book is _____

         _____

    c.    The subject of this book is _____

    d.    The publisher of this book is _____

    e.    This book has _____ pages.

    f.    The (call) number of this book is _____

    g.    (Circle the correct answer)  This book is:  fiction, nonfiction,

         story collection, biography, reference.

2. Put the following fiction books in order as they would be on the

   shelves:

| F | F | F | F | F | F | F | F | F | F |
|---|---|---|---|---|---|---|---|---|---|
| She | Wal | Cal | Tre | Fly | Bro | Gib | Bla | Nec | Jon |

   ___   ___   ___   ___   ___   ___   ___   <u>1</u>   ___   ___

3.  Put the following Dewey Decimal numbers in order as you would find

    them on the shelves:

    | 412 | 229 | 808.8 | 131 | 970.3 | 581 | 792 | 336.4 | 636.7 | 811 |
    |-----|-----|-------|-----|-------|-----|-----|-------|-------|-----|
    | Cab | Mat | Bel   | Tra | Cha   | Swe | And | Lew   | Dra   | Ste |

    ___   ___   ___   ___   ___   ___   ___   ___   ___   ___

4.  Look in the card catalog for the subject, BIRDS.  How many books do

    we have with this exact subject heading? _____

5.  Find 3 titles of books under BIRDS in our card catalog.  Write the

    name of the author, the title of the book, and the call number.  If

    you can locate the book on the shelves, put a check on the line.

| AUTHOR | TITLE | CALL NO. | I found the book |
|--------|-------|----------|------------------|
| _____ | _____ | _____ | _____ |
| _____ | _____ | _____ | _____ |
| _____ | _____ | _____ | _____ |

# 4 ENCYCLOPEDIAS

The most basic research is usually done in an encyclopedia and some advanced research often begins with background reference from an encyclopedia. Every educated person needs to know how to effectively and efficiently locate information in an encyclopedia.

In this kit, the student will be introduced to the various types of encyclopedias and will discover the physical arrangement of subjects in a set of encyclopedias. The student will become familiar with index arrangement and will understand the relationship of the index entry to the subject text through a detailed analysis. The student will learn to utilize the material located within the subject text, material located in a related article, and "see" references.

## Materials Needed:

1 Set of encyclopedias (Sample used: *The World Book Encyclopedia*)
6 Colored pencils (yellow, blue, green, red, orange, and brown)
1 Felt-tip pen (black)
1 Two- or three-ring notebook binder
1 Blank cassette tape
2 Mimeo or ditto masters.

## Preparing the Visual Book:

1. Select subjects to be used:
   a. Main subject
   b. "See also" subject
   c. "See" subject.
2. Use a copy machine to reproduce the following encyclopedia pages:
   a. Two index pages (*see* figs. 18 and 19).
   b. A pictured article complete on one or two pages. Make two copies of each page (*see* figs. 21, 22, 23, and 24).
   c. A "see also" page containing information on the chosen subject (*see* fig. 26).
3. Trim pages and mount on 8½" x 11" paper.
4. If desired, copy mounted pages to eliminate loose edges.
5. Type the following:
   a. Single subject entry as it appears in the index (*see* fig. 20)
   b. Entire subject entry as it appears in the index (*see* fig. 25)
   c. "See" subject as it appears in the index (*see* fig. 27).
6. Mark and label each page as shown in figures 18–27.
7. Laminate the pages or insert into plastic protective sheaths for durability.
8. Punch two or three holes in each page. Be sure

pages which are shown as being face to face are in correct position before punching.

9. Put illustrations (figs. 18–27) into notebook binder in sequence indicated by numerical order. Be careful that facing pages are correctly positioned.

# Preparing the Script:

1. Select an encyclopedia set.
2. Read the script and select and/or substitute the terminology congruent with that used in your library/media center.
3. Choose your own subject samples or copy those used in the illustrations in this manual. If you are using other examples, make corresponding changes in the script.
4. Select Option 1A or 1B.
5. Decide if Options 2–3, 4, and 5 fit the encyclopedia set you are using. Mark options to be used in script.
6. Proofread the script to correct oversights or errors.
7. Record the script onto the blank cassette tape.

# Preparing the Worksheet:

1. Type the worksheet exactly as it is written

or

2. Substitute your own questions to fit the encyclopedia set you are using.

# Preparing for Student Use:

1. Put a chair in front of a table large enough to hold a set of encyclopedias.

2. Arrange the entire set of encyclopedias between a pair of bookends.
3. Put the recorded tape cassette into a cassette player with earphones.
4. Give the student the visual book.

# Script

Today, you are going to learn to use an encyclopedia. When you are doing research, an encyclopedia is a good place to begin. Encyclopedias contain much information and it is important that you know how to get the most from them.

There are two types of encyclopedias: general encyclopedias and special encyclopedias. General encyclopedias have some information on almost all subjects. Special encyclopedias have more information on one special subject, such as (science, animals, people, *name any others you wish*).

You will learn about general encyclopedias in this lesson. When you have learned how to use a general encyclopedia, you will be able to use a special encyclopedia in the same way.

There are many general encyclopedias, but our school does not have all of them. The sets which we have in our (library/media center) are (*name your general encyclopedia sets*). The encyclopedias are located (*describe the location*).

I have placed a set of the (*World Book*) encyclopedia on the table in front of you. A set of encyclopedias is made up of many books. Each book in a set is called a volume. Look at the encyclopedia set in front of you. Each volume is marked with (a letter or letters of the alphabet).

The subjects in each volume are in alphabetical order. All the subjects in each volume will (begin with the letter on the spine or come alphabetically between the letters on the spine). These (letters) are the guides for each volume. The first volume of the (*World Book*) is labeled (A). This means that all of the subjects found in this volume (begin with the letter [A]).

Begin your encyclopedia research by looking for your subject in the index. The index is usually found in the last volume of the encyclopedia set. The (*World Book*), which you will be using today, has the index in the last volume, number (22). The index is a list of all subject headings that are found in the set of encyclopedias.

Turn to pages 1 and 2 (figs. 18 and 19) in your booklet. Here is an example of two index pages as they look in the index volume. Guide words are written at the top of each page. The guide words have been shaded yellow in your booklet. The guide on the left, (Three-race theory), refers to the first subject heading on the page. A line has been drawn from the guide to the subject heading to show you that they are exactly the same.

The guide on the right, (Tigris River), has also been colored yellow. This guide refers to the last subject entry on the index page. A line has been drawn to show you that the subject heading is exactly the same as the guide.

*OPTION 1A: Two index pages used as one*
These two pages are used together. The guide words tell you the first subject heading on the left hand page and the last subject heading on the right hand page. All of the subjects listed on these two pages will come alphabetically between these guide words.

*OPTION 1B: Individual index pages*
Each page in the index has guide words for the first and last subject heading on that page. All of the subjects on each page will come alphabetically between these guide words.
[End of Option 1]

Turn to page 3 (fig. 20) in your booklet. This is an actual subject entry from the index of our encyclopedia. The subject is (Tiger).

*OPTION 2: Descriptive qualifier*
Following the subject heading is a brief description of this subject, A (tiger) is (a wild cat).
[End of Option 2]

Next, you are told the volume number and the exact page on which you will find the encyclopedia article about (tigers). For the subject (Tiger), you would locate volume (T). Then you would turn to page (222). The index also tells you that this article about (tigers) has (pictures and a map).

Now turn to pages 4 and 5 (figs. 21 and 22) in

your booklet. Here is a copy of the encyclopedia article about (tigers). This is the subject you saw in the index sample. I have typed the information given in the index at the top of the article so you can compare the information in the index with the article itself. The subject used in the index was (Tiger), and this is the subject heading of the article. The subject heading used in the index and for the encyclopedia article have been colored yellow to show you that they are exactly the same.

*OPTION 3: To be used if Option 2 was selected*
Next, the index told you that (a tiger) is (a wild cat). This description is not repeated in these exact words in the article itself. The words used in the article to describe (the tiger) are underlined in the first paragraph. The article then goes on to give more complete information about what (a tiger) is.
[End of Option 3]

The index told you to use volume (T). Volume (T) is the volume in which this article about (tigers) is found because (tiger) (begins with a T). The index also told you that the article would be found on page (222). The page shown here is page (222). A line shows you that the page number given in the index is the page on which the article is located. The pictures listed in the index can be seen on these pages. (The map is on page [223].)

Turn to pages 6 and 7 (figs. 23 and 24) in your booklet. Here is the same article about (tigers). Notice that there are guide words at the top of the encyclopedia pages. The guide words have been colored blue. (Tiger) is the first encyclopedia article on the (left-hand) page so (Tiger) is used as the guide. The last article on the (right-hand) page is about (the tiger lily) so (Tiger Lily) is the guide. Lines have been drawn from the guides to the entries to show you how they are used. (*Pause*) Now find the subject heading for (Tiger). (*Pause*)

Notice that the main subject heading (TIGER) is in capital letters. The article about (the tiger) begins immediately after the subject heading. The section following the main subject heading gives general information about the subject (Tiger). Sometimes an article will have subheadings where you can read more specific information about some part of your subject. The subheadings for the subject (Tiger) have

912  **Three-race theory**—*(Color yellow)*

Chemistry (Chemistry in Medicine) C:319
**Three-race theory** [anthropology]
Races, Human (The Three-Race Theory)
*(Color yellow)*  R:52
Asia (Racial Groups) A:736
**Three Rivers** [Quebec]
Trois-Rivières T:366
**Three Rivers Art Festival**
Pittsburgh (The Arts) P:459
**Three Rivers Stadium**
Pittsburgh (Sports) P:459
*Three Sad Tigers* [book by Cabrera Infante]
Latin-American Literature (Recent
Developments) L:103
**Three Sisters** [mountain, Oregon]
Oregon (Land Regions) O:639
*Three Sisters, The* [play by Chekhov]
Russian Literature (Late Realism) R:534;
*picture on* R:530
*Three Soldiers* [book by Dos Passos]
Dos Passos, John D:257
**Three-spined stickleback** [fish]
Instinct I:226
**Three states, Law of the** [philosophy]
Comte, Auguste Ci:746
*Three Tales* [stories by Flaubert]
Flaubert, Gustave F:203
**Three-way bulb**
Electric Light *picture on* E:131
**Three Wise Men** [Biblical figures]
Magi M:44
*Three Women* [painting by Léger]
Painting (Cubism) P:76a-76b *with picture*
*Threepenny Opera, The* [musical]
Blitzstein, Marc B:321
Brecht, Bertolt B:483
Drama *picture on* D:274
Opera (The Search for New Forms) O:600
Weill, Kurt W:155
**"Threnody"** [poem by Emerson]
Emerson, Ralph Waldo (His Life) E:208
*Thresher* [submarine]
Shipwreck (table) S:349
**Thresher shark** [fish]
Shark (Kinds of Sharks) S:301-302 *with
picture*
**Threshing** [agriculture]
Threshing Machine T:208
Combine Ci:699
Flail F:198
Rice (Harvesting and Threshing) R:301 *with
picture*
**Threshing machine** T:208 *with picture*
Agriculture (The Invention of New Farm
Equipment) A:146b *with picture*
Flail F:198
Wheat (Development of Modern Tools)
W:229-230 *with picture*
**Threshold** [architecture]
House (Interior Construction) H:347-350
**Threshold** [physiology]
Allergy (The Allergic Threshold) A:358
**Thrift** *See* Savings *in this index*
**Thrift** [plant]
Statice So:685
**Thrips** [insect] T:208 *with picture*
Insect (table) I:222p
**Throat** [anatomy] T:208
Human Body *diagram on* H:378
**Throatlatch**
Harness *diagram on* H:65
**Throckmorton, James W.** [American
political leader]
Texas (table) T:164
**Thrombin** [enzyme]
Blood (Blood Clotting) B:326
**Thrombophlebitis** [disorder]
Phlebitis P:354
**Thromboplastin**
Blood (Blood Clotting) B:326
**Thrombosis** [disorder]
Blood (Blood Clotting) B:326-327
Coronary Thrombosis Ci:848
**Thrombus** [physiology]
Heart (Arteriosclerosis) H:137-138 *with
diagram*
**Throne**
Furniture (India) F:498; *picture on* F:496
New Brunswick *picture on* N:160
Parliament *picture on* P:154

**Throne, The** [government]
Great Britain (The Monarchy) G:328
**Thrones** [religion]
Angel A:437
**Throop, Enos T.** [American political leader]
New York (table) N:257
**Throstle** [machine]
Industrial Revolution (Spinning Machines)
I:189
**Throttle**
Airplane (Basic Movements and Controls)
A:223
Carburetor (The Throttle Valve) C:170
*Through the Looking-Glass* [book by Carroll]
Carroll, Lewis C:185
Literature for Children (The Rise of
Illustration) L:323; (Bibliography) L:336
*with picture*
Tenniel, Sir John T:126
*Through the Mackenzie Basin* [book by
Mair]
Mair, Charles M:78
**Through truss bridge**
Bridge (Truss Bridges) B:493
**Throw-in**
Soccer (Restarts) So:448b
**Throwing**
Silk (Throwing) S:380
Track and Field (Field Events) T:278; (World
Track and Field Records) T:281
**Throwing down the gauntlet**
Gauntlet G:70
Glove G:225
**Throwing stick** *See* Boomerang *in this index*
**Thrush** [bird] T:209 *with pictures*
Bird (Birds of Inland Waters and Marshes)
B:262 *with picture*
**Thrush** [disease] T:209
Fungus Disease (Diseases of Human Beings
and Animals) F:486
Horse (Medical Care) H:322
**Thrust** [architecture]
Arch A:555
*Thrust* [painting by Gottlieb]
Gottlieb, Adolph *picture on* G:270
**Thrust** [physics]
Airplane (How an Airplane Flies) A:221 *with
diagram;* (Drag and Thrust) A:222 *with
diagrams*
Airship (Lift and Thrust) A:240
Jet Propulsion (Thrust) J:88
Rocket (How Rockets Work) R:357
Space Travel (table) So:563; (Overcoming
Gravity) So:564
**Thrym** [Norse mythology]
Thor T:203
**Thucydides** [Greek historian] T:210
Greek Literature (Prose Literature) G:371
History (Ancient Times) H:234
Orators and Oratory (Classical Orators)
O:618
**Thug** [history of India] T:210
**Thuggee** [crime]
Thug T:210
**Thule** [Greenland] T:210
Greenland (History) G:378
Rasmussen, Knud Johan Victor R:140
**Thule** [ancient literature]
Thulium T:210
Ultima Thule U:7
**Thulium** [element] T:210
**Thumb** [anatomy]
Hand H:37 *with picture*
Monkey (Hands and Feet) M:606a
**Thumb, Tom** *See* Stratton, Charles Sherwood
*in this index*
**Thumb knot**
Knots, Hitches, and Splices K:282 *with
diagram*
**Thumb ring** [ornament]
Ring (Rings Worn as Ornaments) R:319
**Thumper truck**
Petroleum (Geophysical Studies) P:298-299
*with picture*
**Thun, Lake of** [Switzerland]
Lake of Thun L:43
**Thunder** [weather] T:210 *with diagram*
Lightning (How Lightning Produces Thunder)
L:263
Weather (Storms) W:132-132a

**Thunder Bay** [Ontario] T:211
Ontario (Shoreline and Coastline) O:586d;
*picture on* O:587
**Thunder Hole**
Maine *picture on* M:73
**Thunder plant**
Houseleek H:355 *with picture*
**Thunder pumper** [bird]
Bittern B:303
**Thunderbird Park** [Victoria]
British Columbia (Places to Visit) B:512-
513; *picture on* B:505
**Thunderbirds** [organization]
Air Force, United States *picture on* A:176
**Thunderbolt** [airplane]
Air Force *picture on* A:172
World War II (The Allied Air Offensive)
W:395
**Thunderbolt** [mythology]
Jupiter J:164
**Thunderchief** [airplane]
Air Force, United States *picture on* A:178
*Thunderhead* [book by O'Hara]
O'Hara, Mary O:515
**Thunderhead** [weather]
Cloud (Clouds at More Than One Height)
Ci:561
**Thunderstorm** [weather]
Cloud (Storms) Ci:561
Hail H:8
Weather (Storms) W:132 *with picture*
**Thurber, James** [American author] T:211
*with picture*
American Literature (Short Story Writers
and Humorists) A:402-403
Fable F:3
*Thurber Carnival, The* [book by Thurber]
Thurber, James T:211 *with picture*
**Thurman, Allen Granberry** [American
political leader] T:211
Harrison, Benjamin (Election of 1888) H:74
**Thurmond, Strom** [American political leader]
T:211
Filibustering F:101
South Carolina (table) So:526g; (The Mid-
1900's) So:526h
**Thursday** T:212
**Thurston, Howard** [American magician]
Magician (Illusions) M:48
**Thurstone, Louis Leon** [American
psychologist] T:212
*Thus Spake Zarathustra* [book by
Nietzsche]
Nietzsche, Friedrich N:323
**Thutmose II** [king of ancient Egypt]
Thutmose III T:212
**Thutmose III** [king of ancient Egypt] T:212
Egypt, Ancient (The Early New Kingdom)
E:99
**Thyborøn Canal**
Denmark (Land Regions) D:118
**Thye, Edward J.** [American political leader]
Minnesota (table) M:509
**Thylacine** [animal]
Tasmanian Tiger T:40 *with picture*
**Thyme** [plant] T:212
**Thymine** [biochemistry]
Cell (DNA–The Wondrous Ladder) C:250j
Heredity (DNA) H:193
Nucleic Acid N:449
**Thymol** [medication]
Thyme T:212
**Thymosin** [physiology]
Thymus T:212
**Thymus** [anatomy] T:212 *with diagram*
Blood (Lymphocytes) B:326
Gland (Glandlike Structures) G:197
**Thymus derived cell** [physiology]
Thymus T:212
**Thyratron**
Electronics (Rectifying Electric Current)
E:162
Vacuum Tube (Kinds of Vacuum Tubes)
V:202-202a
**Thyroid artery** [anatomy]
Human Body *diagram on* H:378
**Thyroid cartilage** [anatomy]
Larynx L:79 *with diagram*
**Thyroid gland** [anatomy] T:212 *with diagram*
Cretinism Ci:906

FIG. 18.  Left-hand page of encyclopedia index with subject entry guide

Gland (table) G:197
Goiter G:238
Hormone (Metabolic Hormones) H:302
Human Body *diagram on* H:378
Kocher, Emil Theodor K:287
Metabolism (Basal Metabolism) M:348
Parathyroid Gland P:135
Radioactivity (In Medicine) R:95
**Thyroid stimulating hormone**
Hormone (Endocrine Control Hormones) H:303
**Thyroxine** [hormone]
Thyroid Gland T:212
Cretinism Ci:906
Hormone (Metabolic Hormones) H:302
Kendall, Edward Calvin K:212
**Thyrsus** [botany]
Inflorescence I:206; *picture on* I:205
**Thysanoptera** [entomology]
Insect (table) I:222p
Thrips T:208 *with picture*
**Thysanura** [entomology]
Insect (table) I:222o; *picture on* I:218
**Thyssen** [company]
Manufacturing (table) M:128
**Ti**
Titanium T:235
*Ti Chau* [newssheet]
Journalism (The First Newspapers) J:138
*Ti-pao*
Newspaper (History) N:304
**Tiahuanaco Indians** [American Indians]
Bolivia (Early Days) B:356-357
**Tiahuanaco Museum**
Bolivia (What to See and Do in Bolivia) B:356
**Tiber River** [Italy] T:213
Romulus and Remus R:410
**Tiberias, Sea of**
Sea of Galilee S:210 *with maps*
**Tiberius** [Roman emperor] T:213
Caligula C:55
Denarius *picture on* D:113
**Tiberius Claudius Nero**
Tiberius T:213
**Tibesti Massif** [region, Chad]
Sahara (Land and Climate) S:21
**Tibet** T:214 *with picture and map*
Asia (Way of Life in Central Asia) A:755;
(The People) A:755; (Religions) A:755;
(Life in Tibet) A:755; *picture on* A:737
China (Nationalities) C:382-383 *with map;*
(The Tibetan Highlands) C:390c
Dalai Lama D:8
Funeral Customs (The Funeral) F:483
Painting (Indian Painting) P:46 *with picture*
Shelter (In Asia) S:318
T'ang Dynasty (The Middle Years) T:20f
**Tibetan terrier** [dog] T:216 *with picture*
Dog *picture on* D:229
**Tibia** [anatomy]
Human Body *diagram on* H:378
Knee K:270 *with diagram*
Leg (The Leg) L:159 *with diagram*
**Tibullus** [Roman author]
Latin Literature (The Age of Augustus) L:106
**Tic** [disorder] T:216
Neuralgia N:138
**Tic douloureux** [disorder]
Neuralgia N:138
**Tichenor, Isaac** [American political leader]
Vermont (table) V:268f
**Ticino** [canton, Switzerland]
Switzerland *picture on* So:840d
**Ticino River** [Italy-Switzerland]
Pavia P:179
Switzerland (Rivers) So:840d
**Ticinum**
Pavia P:179
**Tick** [animal] T:216 *with pictures*
See also Mite *in this index*
Dog (Medical Care) D:230b
Parasite (Animal Parasites) P:134 *with picture*
Relapsing Fever R:201
**Tick fever** [disease] T:217
**Tick-Licker** [gun]
Boone, Daniel (His Personality) B:388 *with picture*

**Tickbird** [bird] T:217
**Ticker** *See* Stock ticker *in this index*
**Ticker, Reuben**
Tucker, Richard T:392
**Ticker tape**
Stock Ticker So:710
**Ticket agent** [career]
Airport (Airline Passenger Services) A:236;
*picture on* A:232
**Ticking** [fabric] T:217
**Ticknor, George** [American scholar] T:217
**Tickseed** [plant]
Coreopsis Ci:831 *with picture*
*Ticonderoga* [ship]
Vermont (Places to Visit) V:264-265 *with picture*
**Ticonderoga, Battle of** [1775]
Allen, Ethan A:355
Arnold, Benedict (A Courageous Soldier) A:706
Fort Ticonderoga F:359
**Tidal air** [physiology]
Respiration (Capacity of the Lungs) R:242
**Tidal Basin** [Washington, D.C.]
Washington, D.C. (The National Mall) W:64-65; *picture on* W:66; *map on* W:68
**Tidal current** [ocean]
Tide (High Tides and Low Tides) T:220
**Tidal power plant**
Ocean (Harnessing the Sea's Energy) O:498e
**Tidal theory** [geology]
Earth (The Birth of the Solar System) E:16b
**Tidal wave** T:217
Flood (Seacoast Floods) F:210
Ocean (Ocean Waves) O:498b
**Tide** [air]
Tide (Tides in the Air) T:220
Air (Air Movement) A:156
**Tide** [water] T:218 *with pictures*
Bore B:399
Earth (The Earth's Gravity) E:15
Energy Supply (Tidal Energy) E:226c
Moon (The Moon and Tides) M:647
Ocean (The Tides) O:498c; (Why Study the Sea?) O:498f-499
Seashore S:191
*Tide and Current Tables* [publication]
National Ocean Survey N:41
**Tide-pool johnny** [fish]
Sculpin S:191
**Tidelands** [region, U.S.]
Petroleum (Postwar Developments) P:310
Texas (The Mid-1900's) T:163-164
**Tidewater**
Virginia (Land Regions) V:325-326
**Tidewater aristocracy**
Virginia (Royal Governors and Cromwell) V:328d-328e
*Tidings Brought to Mary* [play by Claudel]
Claudel, Paul Ci:502
**Tie** [music] T:220
**Tie** [railroad]
Railroad (The Rails and Crossties) R:107
**Tie-down roping**
Rodeo (All-Girl Rodeos) R:369-370
**Tie dyeing** [handicraft] T:220
**Tie plate** [construction]
Railroad (The Rails and Crossties) R:107
**Tie-up** [wrestling]
Wrestling *picture on* W:418
**Tied arch bridge**
Bridge (Arch Bridges) B:493
**Tiemann, Norbert T.** [American political leader]
Nebraska (table) N:106
**Tien An Men**
Peking (The City) P:203 *with map*
**Tien Shan** [mountains, Asia] T:220
China (The Sinkiang-Mongolian Uplands) C:390c
**Tientsin** [China] T:221
**Tientsin, Treaty of** [1858]
Elgin, Earl of E:184
**Tiepolo, Giovanni Battista** [Italian painter] T:221
Painting (Painting as Decoration) P:33 *with picture*                    (Color yellow)
**Tiepolo, Giovanni Domenico** [Italian painter]
Mythology *picture on* M:819

**Tierce** [unit of measure]
Weights and Measures (table: Miscellaneous Weights and Measures) W:150
**Tiergarten, The** [park, Berlin]
Berlin (A New City) B:204-204a
**Tierra del Fuego** [islands, Argentina-Chile] T:221 *with maps*
Argentina (Land Regions) A:614
Chile *picture on* C:366
Clothing Ci:530
**Tietê River** [Brazil]
São Paulo (The City) S:104b
**Tiffany, Charles Lewis** [American businessman] T:221
**Tiffany, Louis Comfort** [American artist] T:221 *with portrait*
Art Nouveau A:714
Glass *picture on* G:208
Glassware (Tiffany Favrile Glass) G:214
Stained Glass (Decline and Revival) So:647
**Tiffany diamond**
Diamond *picture on* D:147
**Tiffany Favrile glass**
Glassware (Tiffany Favrile Glass) G:214
Tiffany, Louis Comfort T:221
**Tiffin, Edward** [American political leader]
Ohio (Statehood) O:532e; (table) O:533
**Tiflis** *See* Tbilisi *in this index*
**Tift College** U:160
**Tiger** [wild cat] T:222 *with pictures and map*
Animal *picture on* A:446
Circus *picture on* Ci:437
Mammal *picture on* M:93
Zoo *picture on* Z:504
**Tiger, Dick** [Nigerian boxer]
Boxing (Light Heavyweights) B:440;
(Middleweights) B:440
**"Tiger, The"** [poem by Blake]
Blake, William B:314
**Tiger beetle**
Beetle (Kinds of Beetles) B:170
Insect *picture on* I:221
**Tiger cat** [fur]
Serval S:249
**Tiger cat** [marsupial]
Native Cat N:51
**Tiger cat** [wild cat]
Ocelot O:504 *with picture*
Serval S:249
**Tiger-Cats, Hamilton**
Football (Canadian Football League) F:320
**Tiger cowrie**
Shell *pictures on* S:310b
*Tiger-Lilies* [book by Lanier]
Lanier, Sidney L:67
**Tiger lily** [plant] T:223
**Tiger of France**
Clemenceau, Georges Ci:507
**Tiger Stadium** [Baton Rouge]
Stadium (table) So:644b
**Tiger swallowtail** [insect]
Butterfly *picture on* B:620
**Tigers, Detroit**
Baseball (table) B:98
Detroit (Sports) D:137
*Tiger's Whisker and Other Tales and Legends from Asia and the Pacific, The* [book by Courlander]
Literature for Children (Bibliography) L:333
**Tight money policy**
Interest (Government Policy) I:245
**Tight seat** [furniture]
Upholstery (How Furniture Is Upholstered) U:168
**Tiglath-pileser I** [king of Assyria] T:224
**Tiglath-pileser II** [king of Assyria] T:224
**Tiglath-pileser III** [king of Assyria] T:224
Assyria (History) A:787
**Tiglon** [wild cat]
Lion (Cubs) L:299
**Tignish** [Prince Edward Island]
Prince Edward Island *picture on* P:691
**Tigon** [wild cat]
Lion (Cubs) L:299
**Tigress** [wild cat]
Tiger (The Body of a Tiger) T:222 *with picture;* (The Life of a Tiger) T:223
**Tigris-Euphrates Valley** [region, Iraq]
City (Ancient Cities) Ci:451
**Tigris River** [Iraq-Turkey] T:224

FIG. 19.   Right-hand page of encyclopedia index with subject entry guide

Reprinted from *The World Book Encyclopedia*, Index: 913, by permission of the publisher. Copyright © 1981 by World Book-Childcraft International, Inc.

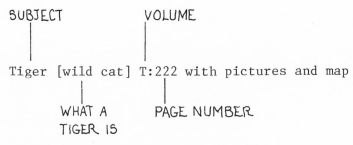

FIG. 20.    Encyclopedia index entry

been colored green. The subheadings are (The Body of a Tiger, How a Tiger Hunts, and The Life of a Tiger). Subheadings will help you find specific information about your subject.

*OPTION 4: Facts in brief*

Some important facts about (the tiger) are found in a box on page (222) of the (*World Book*) article. A red line has been drawn around this box to draw your attention to it. If you need only a few facts, you may find what you need in this section. Usually, however, you will need or want to read the entire article since the information in the box is very brief.
[End of Option 4]


At the very end of the article about (tigers), you will see the name of the author who wrote this article for the encyclopedia. The author's name has been colored orange. (George B. Schaller) was the person who wrote the article about (the tiger).


*OPTION 5: Author information*

More information about the author is given on encyclopedia page (222). By reading this section, also colored orange, you can learn why the author was qualified to write this article.
[End of Option 5]


Sometimes suggestions are given at the end of the article to help you find other articles for more information on your subject. This section has been colored brown on your page. The subjects that the (*World Book*) encyclopedia suggests may help you learn more about (the tiger) are (*read the "see also" subject headings*).

Now, you are going to look at this same article in the (*World Book*) which is in front of you. Take as much time as you need to compare the article as it is in your booklet with the one in the encyclopedia itself. When you have finished looking at the article in the encyclopedia, start the tape recorder again and go on. Now, find volume (T) and turn to page (222). That's volume (T). (*Pause*) Page (222). (*Tone*)

Did you find the article just as it was in your booklet? Did you see the different parts of the article that we talked about? (*Pause*) The subject heading? (*Pause*) The guide words? (*Pause*) The subheadings? (*Pause*) The author? (*Pause*) The "see also" subjects? (*Pause*) If you are not sure about these parts of the article, rewind the tape and listen to it again. When you understand the parts of the article, you are ready to go on to page 8 in your booklet.

You should now be looking at page 8 (fig. 25). This page shows the entire index entry for the subject (Tiger). All the articles listed under this subject heading, (tiger), are about (tigers). For instance, if you want to (see a picture of circus tigers), you would look for the article about (the circus) in volume (Ci) on page (437). This subject is underlined in red in your booklet.

Turn to page 9 (fig. 26) in your booklet. (*Pause*) Encyclopedia page (437) was the page given in the index for a (picture of tigers in the circus). Notice that page (437) is not the page on which the article about (the circus) begins, but it is the page that has (a picture of circus tigers). If you had looked in this volume without using the index, you would have had to hunt for this page. The index made it easy to find exactly the page you needed.

Some articles in the encyclopedia are many pages long. You will save a lot of time if you always begin by looking in the index.

**TIGER**
(Color yellow)

`Tiger [wild cat] T:222 with picture`

Ylla, Rapho Guillumette

**The Tiger's Coloration** helps conceal the animal in its natural surroundings. This female tiger could easily go unseen because her stripes blend with the tall grasses.

(Color yellow)

**TIGER** is the largest member of the cat family. People admire the tiger for its strength and beauty, but they fear it because it has been known to kill and eat human beings. Yet almost all wild tigers avoid people. Probably only 3 or 4 of every 1,000 tigers ever eat people, and some of these are sick or wounded animals that can no longer hunt large prey.

Wild tigers are found only in Asia. Until the 1800's, many lived throughout most of the southern half of the continent. Tigers still live in some of this area, but only a few are left. People have greatly reduced the number of tigers by hunting them and by clearing the forests in which they lived. Today, wildlife experts consider the tiger an endangered species.

Tigers can live in almost any climate. They need only shade, water, and prey. They are found in the hot rain forests of Malaya, the dry thorn woods of India, and the cold, snowy spruce forests of Manchuria. They also live in oak woods, tall grasslands, swamps, and marshes. Tigers prefer to be in the shadows and seldom go into open country as lions do. Many tigers also live in zoos. In the past, wild tigers were captured for zoos. Today, enough tigers for zoos are born in captivity.

**The Body of a Tiger.** Adult male tigers weigh about 420 pounds (191 kilograms) and are 9 feet (2.7 meters) long, including a 3-foot (0.9-meter) tail. Tigresses weigh about 300 pounds (136 kilograms) and are 8 feet (2.4

meters) long. The tiger's coat ranges from brownish-yellow to orange-red and is marked by black stripes. The stripes vary greatly in length, width, and spacing. The fur on the throat, belly, and insides of the legs is whitish. Many tigers have a ruff of hair around the sides of the head, but the hair is not so long as the mane of lions. The tigers of Manchuria, where the winters are bitter cold, have long, shaggy, winter coats.

The tiger looks different from the lion because of its stripes and more colorful coat. But the two animals have similar bodies. In fact, tigers and lions have mated in zoos. The offspring are called *tiglons*, *tigons*, or *ligers*.

**How a Tiger Hunts.** Tigers prefer large prey, such as deer, antelope, wild oxen, and wild pigs. Some tigers attack elephant calves. They also eat small prey, such as peafowl, monkeys, tortoises, and frogs. Tigers especially like porcupines, but their quills sometimes stick in a tiger's body and cause painful wounds. In parts of Asia, some tigers prey on domestic cattle and

---
**FACTS IN BRIEF**
---

**Names:** *Male*, tiger; *female*, tigress; *young*, cub.

**Gestation Period:** 98 to 109 days.

**Number of Newborn:** 1 to 6, usually 2 or 3.

**Length of Life:** Up to 20 years.

**Where Found:** Chiefly in Bangladesh, India, Nepal, and Southeast Asia, including Sumatra; also a few in China, Iran, Java, and Korea, and along the Siberian-Manchurian border.

**Scientific Classification:** Tigers belong to the class *Mammalia* and the order *Carnivora*. They are in the cat family, *Felidae*, and the genus *Panthera*. All tigers are of the same species, *P. tigris*.

---

*George B. Schaller, the contributor of this article, is a Research Associate with the New York Zoological Society and the author of* The Deer and the Tiger.

222

---

FIG. 21.    Left-hand text page of encyclopedia

(Color yellow) `Tiger` [wild cat] T:222 with pictures and map    **TIGER LILY**

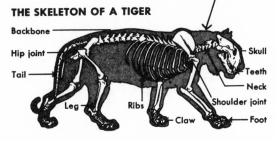

Marc & Evelyne Bernheim, Rapho Guillumette

**The Male Tiger** has heavier patches of fur around its face than the female. This male is taking a dip on a hot day.

**THE SKELETON OF A TIGER**

Backbone
Hip joint
Tail
Skull
Teeth
Neck
Shoulder joint
Leg
Ribs
Claw
Foot

**TIGER TRACKS**

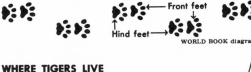

Front feet
Hind feet
WORLD BOOK diagram

**WHERE TIGERS LIVE**

The black areas in the map below show the parts of the world where tigers are found. Most tigers live in southern Asia.

buffalo because man has reduced the number of wildlife.

The tiger usually hunts at night, wandering over animal trails and along stream beds. A tiger depends on its sharp eyes and keen ears, but it may also use its sense of smell. The tiger, waiting in cover, rushes at its prey in a series of bounds. Using its sharp claws, the tiger grasps the victim by the rump or side and pulls it to the ground. The tiger's teeth are well suited both for holding prey and for tearing off chunks of meat.

Tigers are extremely swift for short distances and can leap nearly 30 feet (9 meters). But if a tiger fails to catch its prey quickly, it usually will give up because it soon tires. As long as a week may go by without a successful hunt. After a kill, the tiger drags the *carcass* (dead body) to thick cover, preferably near water. The muscles of the tiger's neck, shoulders, and forelegs are very powerful. A tiger may drag the body of a 500-pound (230-kilogram) young water buffalo ¼ mile (0.4 kilometer). The tiger stays near the carcass until it has eaten everything except the bones and stomach. A tiger may eat 50 pounds (23 kilograms) of meat in a night. A long drink and a nap often follow a meal.

Tigers are good swimmers and may swim across rivers or from one island to another in search of prey. On hot days, they may go into the water to cool off. Tigers can climb trees, but they do not usually do so.

**The Life of a Tiger.** Adult tigers usually live alone, but they are not unfriendly. Two tigers may meet on their nightly rounds, rub heads together in greeting, and then part. Several tigers may share a kill.

Many adult males claim a territory as their own and keep other males out. The territory may cover from 25 to 250 square miles (65 to 647 square kilometers) or more, depending on the amount of prey available. The tiger marks a path with urine and with fluids from glands at the base of the tail. The scent lets other tigers know that the territory is occupied. A male may share his area with one or several females, each wandering alone but aware of one another. Tigers communicate by many sounds, including a roar that can be heard for 2 miles (3 kilometers) or more.

A tigress can bear her first cubs when she is 3½ to 4 years old. The cubs are helpless and weigh about 3 pounds (1.4 kilograms) at birth. Tiger cubs, like kittens, are playful. But their life is hazardous, and about half die before they are a year old. The cubs cannot kill enough for themselves until they are more than a year old. Even then, they cannot kill a large animal. The mother may teach her cubs how to kill by providing a live animal for them to attack. Cubs become independent when about 2 years old.    GEORGE B. SCHALLER

See also ANIMAL (Animals of the Tropical Forests [color picture]); LION; SABER-TOOTHED CAT.

**TIGER CAT** is another name for the moderate-sized wildcats of Africa and the Americas. See MARGAY; OCELOT; SERVAL.

**TIGER LILY** is a tall garden flower that originally grew in eastern Asia. It received its name because it has reddish-orange flowers splashed with black. People in China, Japan, and Korea serve tiger lily bulbs as food.

The stem of the tiger lily is greenish-purple or dark brown, and many grow from 5 to 6 feet (1.5 to 1.8 meters) tall. Tiny black bulblets appear where the long,

**223**

FIG. 22.    Right-hand text page of encyclopedia

TIGER ← GUIDE
(Color blue)

Ylla, Rapho Guillumette

**The Tiger's Coloration** helps conceal the animal in its natural surroundings. This female tiger could easily go unseen because her stripes blend with the tall grasses.

MAIN
SUBJECT ——(Blue line)
HEADING
(Color blue)

**TIGER** is the largest member of the cat family. People admire the tiger for its strength and beauty, but they fear it because it has been known to kill and eat human beings. Yet almost all wild tigers avoid people. Probably only 3 or 4 of every 1,000 tigers ever eat people, and some of these are sick or wounded animals that can no longer hunt large prey.

Wild tigers are found only in Asia. Until the 1800's, many lived throughout most of the southern half of the continent. Tigers still live in some of this area, but only a few are left. People have greatly reduced the number of tigers by hunting them and by clearing the forests in which they lived. Today, wildlife experts consider the tiger an endangered species. (Color green)

Tigers can live in almost any climate. They need only shade, water, and prey. They are found in the hot rain forests of Malaya, the dry thorn woods of India, and the cold, snowy spruce forests of Manchuria. They also live in oak woods, tall grasslands, swamps, and marshes. Tigers prefer to be in the shadows and seldom go into open country as lions do. Many tigers also live in zoos. In the past, wild tigers were captured for zoos. Today, enough tigers for zoos are born in captivity.

SUB- ——→ **The Body of a Tiger.** Adult male tigers weigh about
HEADING 420 pounds (191 kilograms) and are 9 feet (2.7 meters)
(Color green) long, including a 3-foot (0.9-meter) tail. Tigresses weigh about 300 pounds (136 kilograms) and are 8 feet (2.4

AUTHOR INFORMATION (Color orange)

*George B. Schaller, the contributor of this article, is a Research Associate with the New York Zoological Society and the author of* The Deer and the Tiger.

meters) long. The tiger's coat ranges from brownish-yellow to orange-red and is marked by black stripes. The stripes vary greatly in length, width, and spacing. The fur on the throat, belly, and insides of the legs is whitish. Many tigers have a ruff of hair around the sides of the head, but the hair is not so long as the mane of lions. The tigers of Manchuria, where the winters are bitter cold, have long, shaggy, winter coats.

The tiger looks different from the lion because of its stripes and more colorful coat. But the two animals have similar bodies. In fact, tigers and lions have mated in zoos. The offspring are called *tiglons, tigons,* or *ligers.*

**How a Tiger Hunts.** Tigers prefer large prey, such as deer, antelope, wild oxen, and wild pigs. Some tigers attack elephant calves. They also eat small prey, such as peafowl, monkeys, tortoises, and frogs. Tigers especially like porcupines, but their quills sometimes stick in a tiger's body and cause painful wounds. In parts of Asia, some tigers prey on domestic cattle and

─────── **FACTS IN BRIEF** ───────

**Names:** *Male,* tiger; *female,* tigress; *young,* cub.
**Gestation Period:** 98 to 109 days.
**Number of Newborn:** 1 to 6, usually 2 or 3.    (Red outline)
**Length of Life:** Up to 20 years.
**Where Found:** Chiefly in Bangladesh, India, Nepal, and Southeast Asia, including Sumatra; also a few in China, Iran, Java, and Korea, and along the Siberian-Manchurian border.
**Scientific Classification:** Tigers belong to the class *Mammalia* and the order *Carnivora.* They are in the cat family, *Felidae,* and the genus *Panthera.* All tigers are of the same species, *P. tigris.*

222

FIG. 23.   Information elements in an encyclopedia entry

Reprinted from *The World Book Encyclopedia*, T:222, by permission of the publisher. Copyright © 1981 by World Book-Childcraft International, Inc.

Marc & Evelyne Bernheim, Rapho Guillumette

**The Male Tiger** has heavier patches of fur around its face than the female. This male is taking a dip on a hot day.    *(Color green)*

## THE SKELETON OF A TIGER

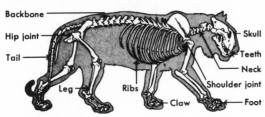

Backbone
Hip joint
Tail
Leg        Ribs
Skull
Teeth
Neck
Shoulder joint
Claw        Foot

## TIGER TRACKS

Front feet
Hind feet
WORLD BOOK diagram

## WHERE TIGERS LIVE

The black areas in the map below show the parts of the world where tigers are found. Most tigers live in southern Asia.

*(Color blue)*

buffalo because man has reduced the number of wildlife.

The tiger usually hunts at night, wandering over animal trails and along stream beds. A tiger depends on its sharp eyes and keen ears, but it may also use its sense of smell. The tiger, waiting in cover, rushes at its prey in a series of bounds. Using its sharp claws, the tiger grasps the victim by the rump or side and pulls it to the ground. The tiger's teeth are well suited both for holding prey and for tearing off chunks of meat.

Tigers are extremely swift for short distances and can leap nearly 30 feet (9 meters). But if a tiger fails to catch its prey quickly, it usually will give up because it soon tires. As long as a week may go by without a successful hunt. After a kill, the tiger drags the *carcass* (dead body) to thick cover, preferably near water. The muscles of the tiger's neck, shoulders, and forelegs are very powerful. A tiger may drag the body of a 500-pound (230-kilogram) young water buffalo ¼ mile (0.4 kilometer). The tiger stays near the carcass until it has eaten everything except the bones and stomach. A tiger may eat 50 pounds (23 kilograms) of meat in a night. A long drink and a nap often follow a meal.

Tigers are good swimmers and may swim across rivers or from one island to another in search of prey. On hot days, they may go into the water to cool off. Tigers can climb trees, but they do not usually do so.

**The Life of a Tiger.** Adult tigers usually live alone, but they are not unfriendly. Two tigers may meet on their nightly rounds, rub heads together in greeting, and then part. Several tigers may share a kill.

Many adult males claim a territory as their own and keep other males out. The territory may cover from 25 to 250 square miles (65 to 647 square kilometers) or more, depending on the amount of prey available. The tiger marks a path with urine and with fluids from glands at the base of the tail. The scent lets other tigers know that the territory is occupied. A male may share his area with one or several females, each wandering alone but aware of one another. Tigers communicate by many sounds, including a roar that can be heard for 2 miles (3 kilometers) or more.

A tigress can bear her first cubs when she is 3½ to 4 years old. The cubs are helpless and weigh about 3 pounds (1.4 kilograms) at birth. Tiger cubs, like kittens, are playful. But their life is hazardous, and about half die before they are a year old. The cubs cannot kill enough for themselves until they are more than a year old. Even then, they cannot kill a large animal. The mother may teach her cubs how to kill by providing a live animal for them to attack. Cubs become independent when about 2 years old.    GEORGE B. SCHALLER

See also ANIMAL (Animals of the Tropical Forests [color picture]); LION; SABER-TOOTHED CAT.

**TIGER CAT** is another name for the moderate-sized wildcats of Africa and the Americas. See MARGAY; OCELOT; SERVAL.

**TIGER LILY** is a tall garden flower that originally grew in eastern Asia. It received its name because it has reddish-orange flowers splashed with black. People in China, Japan, and Korea serve tiger lily bulbs as food.

The stem of the tiger lily is greenish-purple or dark brown, and many grow from 5 to 6 feet (1.5 to 1.8 meters) tall. Tiny black bulblets appear where the long,

SEE ALSO          AUTHOR
(Color brown)        (Color orange) **223**

Fɪɢ. 24.    Additional information elements

**Under the Big Top.** Most circus acts take place in round areas called *rings*. A small circus may have only one or two rings. Large circuses have three rings where three acts go on at the same time. There is so much to see that no one can follow everything that happens in all the rings.

In one ring, elephants stand on their hind legs and dance. In another, trained seals balance big rubber balls on their noses. Trained horses *canter*, or gallop gently, in a circle while riders jump from horse to horse. A family of riders stand on each other's shoulders on the backs of horses cantering side by side around the ring. A lion tamer enters a cage and cracks a whip. The big cats leap onto platforms upon command.

Some performers hang by their teeth from a rope and twirl around and around. Others, called *flyers*, leap through the air from one trapeze to another. They perform daring somersaults in the air before being caught by other members of the act. Other acts feature performers on the high wire, riding bicycles or doing acrobatics.

The circus band plays throughout the show. The band helps keep the acts running on time. By playing faster or slower, or by changing tunes, it signals the performers when to finish the various parts of their acts. The music keeps up the feeling of excitement and pride in the performance that is as old as the circus itself.

Many circus stars have become world famous. Poodles Hanneford and his family combined clowning with skillful bareback riding. Arthur Concello and his wife Antoinette won fame on the flying trapeze. Antoinette Concello became the first woman to perform a triple somersault, the most difficult trapeze stunt. Clyde Beatty and Mabel Stark became known for their acts with wild jungle animals. Gunther Gebel-Williams also gained fame as an animal trainer. Famous circus clowns have included Felix Adler, Otto Griebling, Lou Jacobs, and Emmett Kelly.

Franz Furstner, known as "Unus," stood on top of a pole on one finger. His daughter, Vicki, became famous for doing one-armed swings while hanging from a

Susan Ylvisaker, Jeroboam, Inc.

**Clowns** in funny costumes and comic makeup entertain the audience with their playful antics and humorous stunts. The clowns often perform between acts.

© Michael Philip Manheim

**Daring Aerialists** perform acrobatic feats high above the ground. One member of this team hangs from a trapeze, ready to catch his partner.

Robert H. Glaze, Artstreet

**Wild Animal Acts** provide great excitement for audiences. These tigers do tricks on command from their trainer. To protect the spectators, the tigers perform inside a wire cage.

437

FIG. 26.   Index subentry picture reference

```
Tiger [wild cat] T:222 with pictures and map

  Animal picture on A:446

  Circus picture of Ci:437

  Mammal picture on M:93

  Zoo picture on Z:504
```

FIG. 25.   Encyclopedia index main entry and subentries

Reprinted from *The World Book Encyclopedia*, Index:913, by permission of the publisher. Copyright © 1981 by World Book-Childcraft International, Inc.

```
Sunset

  Twilight T:434

  Astronomy (The Daytime Sky) A:802 with

    picture; (Why the Stars Seem to Move)

    A:  802-803
```

FIG. 27.   Index entry for subject to be found under differing subject entries

Reprinted from *The World Book Encyclopedia*, Index:884, by permission of the publisher. Copyright © 1981 by World Book-Childcraft International, Inc.

Not all subjects are found in the encyclopedia volume in which you think they should be found. Turn to page 10 (fig. 27) in your booklet. (*Pause*) The subject here is (Sunset). No volume or page number is given after this subject heading. Instead, other subjects are listed with the volume and page numbers. (Twilight and Astronomy) are the subjects used in the (*World Book*) encyclopedia for information about (sunsets). Turn to volume (19–T), find page (434), and locate the article about the subject heading (Twilight). That's volume (T). (*Pause*) Page (434). (*Tone*)

As you have been looking at the encyclopedia, you have probably noticed many illustrations. Pictures, maps, diagrams, graphs, and lists are all helpful when you are learning about a subject. Don't forget to look at the illustrations carefully when you are reading an article. You may find exactly what you need in the illustrations.

By now, you may be ready to do the worksheet on encyclopedias. If you feel that you need to review the information, play the tape again or look through your booklet. When you are ready, see (*your name*) for the worksheet. Good luck!

[End of Script]

*WORKSHEET*

1.  Here is an example from the index of the (World Book Encyclopedia).

    Match each part of the sample with the words that tell what it is:

    Elephant [animal] E:178 with pictures

    Ivory I:413

    a.  Elephant            Volume in which the subject, Elephant,

                            is found

    b.  [animal]            Another subject heading with

                                information about elephants

    c.  E:                  Page on which the subject, Ivory, is found

    d.  178                 Description of what an elephant is

    e.  with pictures       Main subject heading

    f.  Ivory               Page on which the article about

                                elephants begins

    g.  I:                  There will be a picture of an

                                elephant in this article

    h.  413                 Volume in which subject, Ivory, is found

2.  Use the index of the (World Book) and find the volume and page

    where you will find the following:

    a.  Mouse           Volume _____ Page _____

    b.  Roadster        Volume _____ Page _____

    c.  Jazz band       Volume _____ Page _____

    d.  Fresh air       Volume _____ Page _____

3.  Use your (World Book) index to find the main article about

    dinosaurs.  Answer the following questions:

    a.   In what volume and on what page will this article begin?

         Volume _____    Page _____

    b.   On what page does the article end? _____

    c.   What is the first subheading of this article?

         _____

    d.   Who is the author of this article?

         _____

    e.   List two other articles in the (World Book) that will give

         you more information about dinosaurs:

         _____

         _____

# 5 CHILDREN'S MAGAZINE GUIDE

*Children's Magazine Guide* is the periodical index most used in elementary school library media centers. This chapter provides a kit for introducing the student to the value of a periodical index and teaches the student to use the *Children's Magazine Guide*.

With this kit, the student will learn the purpose of a periodical index and how to locate periodical articles by subject reference in the index. The student will discover where to find the keys for decoding abbreviations of periodicals and words. The student will examine an index entry in depth and may compare it to the article as it actually appears in the periodical. The student will learn to use "See" and "See Also" references.

*Children's Magazine Guide*, formerly *Subject Index to Children's Magazines*, is in the process of updating and changing its format. Some samples which appear in this chapter may not correspond exactly to the format when you prepare your kit. Make changes accordingly.

## Materials Needed:

1 *Children's Magazine Guide*
7 Colored pencils (blue, red, yellow, green, pink, orange, and brown)
1 Felt-tip pen (black)
1 Two- or three-ring notebook binder
1 Blank cassette tape
1 Periodical with articles and stories
1 Periodical to correspond to fig. 32 (Option 1).

## Preparing the Visual Book:

1. Use a copy machine to transfer the cover, inside cover page, and one index page of *Children's Magazine Guide*.
   a. Cover page (*see* fig. 28):
      1) Draw a circle around the title with black felt-tip pen.
      2) Color the date blue.
      3) Color the volume and number red.
   b. Inside cover page (*see* fig. 29):
      1) Color the heading "Abbreviations of Magazines Indexed," red.
      2) Color one abbreviated title blue (Child D – CHILDREN'S DIGEST).
      3) Color the heading, "Abbreviations," green.
      4) Color the abbreviation (cont. – continued), orange.
   c. Trim each page and mount on type paper.
2. Type one complete entry, including subject heading (*see* fig. 30). Use entry having magazine abbreviation illustrated in fig. 29 (Child D). Color the magazine abbreviation blue.

3. Type another complete entry with a different magazine abbreviation (*see* fig. 31). Color the magazine abbreviation blue.
4. Type a complete entry (*see* fig. 32). Color as follows:
   a. Subject heading—yellow
   b. Title—pink
   c. Author—green
   d. Magazine title—blue
   e. Volume—red
   f. Pages—brown
   g. Date—orange.
5. Type at least two entries for a subject heading (*see* fig. 33). Draw a dotted line to show how entries line up.
6. Type a list of subjects with subheadings (*see* fig. 34).
7. Type a "see" entry (*see* fig. 35).
8. Type a "see also" entry (*see* fig. 36).
9. Laminate the pages or insert into plastic protective sheaths for durability.
10. Punch two or three holes in side of each page.
11. Put illustrations (figs. 28–37) into notebook binder in sequence indicated by numerical order.

# Preparing the Script:

1. Read the script, select, and/or substitute the terminology congruent with that used in your library/media center.
2. Decide whether to use Option 1.
3. If you are using samples other than those used in the illustrations, make changes where necessary in the script.
4. Proofread the script to correct any oversights or errors.
5. Record the script onto the blank cassette tape.

# Preparing the Worksheet:

1. Type the worksheet exactly as it is written

or

2. Substitute other examples for those given and make up your own worksheet.

# Preparing for Student Use:

1. Arrange a table and chair.
2. Put the recorded tape cassette into a cassette player with earphones.
3. Put a copy of a magazine on the table.
4. If using Option 1, put the corresponding magazine on the table.
5. Give the student the sample copy of *Children's Magazine Guide* and the visual book.

# Script

Today, you are going to learn how to find articles and stories in magazines. You have enjoyed reading magazines for fun, but did you know that magazines have another important purpose?

Information in magazines is more up-to-date than information in books. It takes a long time for a book to be written and published and even longer until we get a copy of the book for our (library/media center) here at (*name of school*).

Because it takes so long for us to get a book about current events, you will want to use magazines when you need to find up-to-date information. Pick up the magazine (*name the title*) which is on the table in front of you. Take a few minutes to glance through the magazine and look at the articles and stories in it. (*Tone*)

(*Name of magazine*) has many articles and stories. An article is a short piece of writing on a certain subject. Articles are nonfiction, which means that the information given in them is true. On page (*give page number*) in your magazine, you will see a nonfiction article. Turn to page (*specify*) in (*name of magazine*). (*Tone*) The article, (*give the title*), tells you facts about (*describe*). Some magazines, such as (*National Geographic World*) or (*National Wildlife*), contain mostly nonfiction articles.

Stories are the fiction part of magazines. On page (*give the page number*) of (*name of magazine*), there is an example of a story. Turn to page (*specify*). (*Tone*) (*Title of the story*) is a story about (*describe*). A few magazines, such as (*Plays*), are entirely fiction.

Most of our magazines have both articles and stories in each issue. At (*name of school*), we take (*give number of titles*) magazines. This is the number of the different magazines you will find in our (library/media center). We receive a copy of the titles we take at least once a month during the school year. Our newest magazines are located (*describe the location*). The older copies of these magazines, called back issues, are found (*describe the location*). We save our magazines for (*give number of years*) years.

When you need to find a magazine article on a certain subject, you could start by looking through all of the magazines we have. Hunting for an article in this way would take you a long time and you might never find the article you need. Instead of spending hours trying to find an article by searching through every magazine, you can save a lot of time and trouble by using *Children's Magazine Guide*. *Children's Magazine Guide* will help you find the article or story you need in just a few minutes. Our copies of *Children's Magazine Guide* are located (*describe the location*).

There is a copy of *Children's Magazine Guide* on the table in front of you. You will be using this copy along with the booklet that is also on the table.

Open your booklet to the first page. This is a copy of the cover of *Children's Magazine Guide* (fig. 28). A circle has been drawn around the name. Let's begin by talking about the name itself.

The first word of the title is *Children's*. The word "children's" tells you that the *Children's Magazine Guide* is written especially for children.

The second word of the title is *Magazine*. Magazines are made up of short articles and stories, as you just learned. Some magazines specialize in one subject, such as science or news. Others have a wide variety of subjects. Magazines are published at regular times during the year. Some magazines are printed every month, some are published every week, and some are printed only a few times each year. No matter how often the magazine is printed, it comes out at regular times during the year. Magazines have paper covers and are many different sizes.

Children's magazines have articles and stories that are especially important for young people. There are many, many magazines printed every year. Some are magazines that your parents might read at home, such as (*Ladies Home Journal*) or (*Sports Afield*). There are other magazines that people like doctors, teachers, and scientists read to help them do their work better. Some magazines are printed especially for children and some magazines have articles that are of interest to children and adults. These are the magazines we have at (*name of school*) for you.

The third and last word of the title is *Guide*. A guide is something that helps you find what you are looking for. *Children's Magazine Guide* will lead you to magazine articles that you can use in your school work for assignments or for reading about a subject in which you are especially interested. What all of this means is that *Children's Magazine Guide* has lists of articles and stories that you can find in children's magazines.

Let's see what other information is given on the cover of *Children's Magazine Guide*. Look at the date. It is colored blue. This is the (September 1981) issue of *Children's Magazine Guide*. All magazine articles and stories that are included in this issue will be from magazines that were printed in (September). In this issue, all magazines listed were published in (September 1981).

In red, below the date on the *Children's Magazine Guide* is the volume and number of this issue. This is volume (34) and number (1).

Now, open your copy of *Children's Magazine Guide* to the inside of the cover page. (*Pause*) Turn to page 2 in your booklet. (*Pause*) Page 2

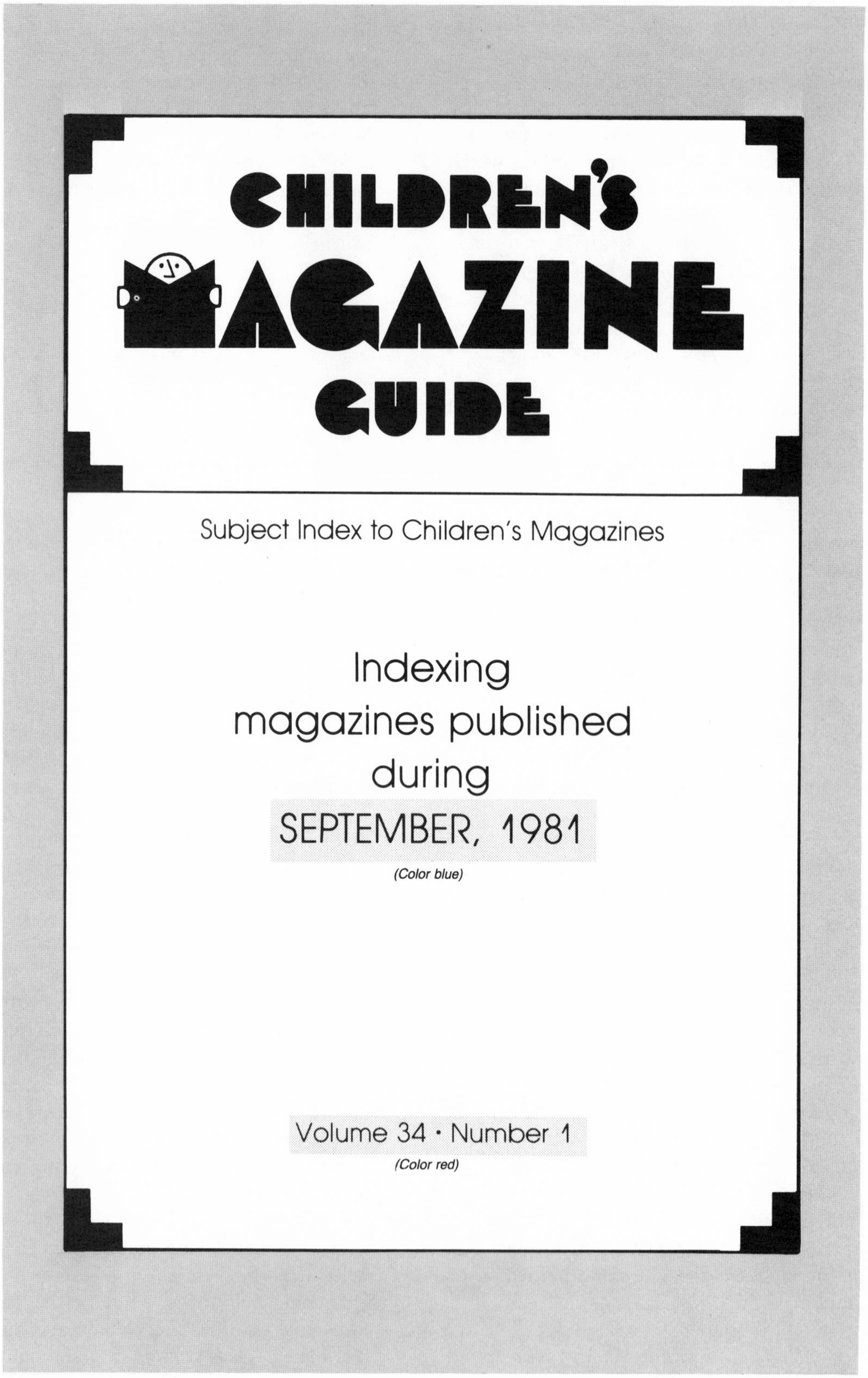
CHILDREN'S MAGAZINE GUIDE

Subject Index to Children's Magazines

Indexing
magazines published
during
SEPTEMBER, 1981

*(Color blue)*

Volume 34 · Number 1

*(Color red)*

FIG. 28. Cover of September 1981 issue

(fig. 29) in your booklet is the same as the inside of the cover of your copy of *Children's Magazine Guide*. This page has information you will need when you use *Children's Magazine Guide*. At the top of the page is a heading, "Abbreviations of Magazines Indexed." The heading is colored red. An abbreviation is a contraction or shortened way to write a word. Some or most of the letters in a word are left out to save space when a word is abbreviated. By looking at this page, you can find what magazine an abbreviation stands for. As an example I have colored one magazine abbreviation blue in your copy. (*Child D*) is the abbreviation used for the magazine (*Children's Digest*).

## ABBREVIATIONS OF MAGAZINES INDEXED
*(Color red)*

Check the magazines your library subscribes to
as a quick reference for users.

☐ Action - SCHOLASTIC ACTION
☐ Art & Man - ART & MAN
☐ Bananas - BANANAS
☐ Beaver - THE BEAVER
☐ Boys' Life - BOYS' LIFE
☐ Career World - CAREER WORLD
☐ Chickadee - CHICKADEE
☑ Child D - CHILDREN'S DIGEST
☐ Child Life - CHILD LIFE    *(Color blue)*
☐ Cobble - COBBLESTONE
☐ Co-ed - CO-ED
☐ Contact - 3-2-1 CONTACT
☐ Cricket - CRICKET
☐ Cur Ev - CURRENT EVENTS
☐ Cur Health - CURRENT HEALTH 1
☐ Cur Sci - CURRENT SCIENCE
☐ Curious Nat - CURIOUS NATURALIST
☐ Dyn - DYNAMITE
☐ Ebony Jr - EBONY JR!
☐ Explorer - SCHOLASTIC NEWS
    EXPLORER
☐ Extra - KNOW YOUR WORLD EXTRA
☐ Eye - MY WEEKLY READER EYE
☐ Highlights - HIGHLIGHTS FOR
    CHILDREN
☐ Horn Bk - HORN BOOK
☐ Humpty D - HUMPTY DUMPTY'S
    MAGAZINE FOR LITTLE
    CHILDREN
☐ Insports - INSPORTS
☐ Instr - INSTRUCTOR
☐ Jack & Jill - JACK & JILL
☐ Jr Schol - JUNIOR SCHOLASTIC
☐ Kind - KIND
☐ Learn - LEARNING
☐ Nat Canada - NATURE CANADA

☐ Nat Geog - NATIONAL GEOGRAPHIC
    MAGAZINE
☐ Nat Wildlife - NATIONAL WILDLIFE
☐ News Cit - SCHOLASTIC NEWS
    CITIZEN
☐ News Trails - SCHOLASTIC NEWS
    TRAILS
☐ Newstime - SCHOLASTIC NEWSTIME
☐ Odyssey - ODYSSEY
☐ Owl - OWL MAGAZINE
☐ Parade - MY WEEKLY READER
    NEWS PARADE
☐ Pen Pow - PENNY POWER
☐ Pict Ed - PICTORIAL EDUCATION
☐ Playmate - CHILDREN'S PLAYMATE
☐ Plays - PLAYS
☐ Pop Mech - POPULAR MECHANICS
☐ Pop Sci - POPULAR SCIENCE
☐ Ranger Rick - RANGER RICK'S
    NATURE MAGAZINE
☐ Read - READ
☐ Sci World - SCIENCE WORLD
☐ Sciland - SCIENCELAND
☐ Search - SCHOLASTIC SEARCH
☐ Sprint - SCHOLASTIC SPRINT
☐ Sr Schol - SENIOR SCHOLASTIC
☐ Sr Wkly R - SENIOR WEEKLY
    READER
☐ Wee Wisdom - WEE WISDOM
☐ World - NATIONAL GEOGRAPHIC
    WORLD
☐ Young Ath - YOUNG ATHLETE
☐ Young Miss - YOUNG MISS
☐ YYW - YOU AND YOUR WORLD
☐ Zoonooz - ZOONOOZ

## ABBREVIATIONS
*(Color green)*

| | | |
|---|---|---|
| bc - cover | fc - front cover | supp - supplement |
| concl. - conclusion | no. - number | trans. - translator |
| cont. - continued | p - page | + - cont. on later pages |
| ed. - editor    *(Color orange)* | pt - part | ... - words omitted |

FIG. 29.   Abbreviations used for magazines indexed

Keep your copy of *Children's Magazine Guide* open to this inside cover page and turn to page 3 (fig. 30) in your booklet. (*Pause*) Here is an example of how a magazine abbreviation is used in the index itself. The abbreviation of the magazine, (*Child D*), is colored blue again to help you. From looking at the inside cover page of *Children's Magazine Guide*, you know that (*Child D*) is the abbreviation for (*Children's Digest*). Let's try another title. Turn to page 4 (fig. 31) in your booklet. (*Pause*) By looking in the list of abbreviations on the inside cover page of your copy of *Children's Magazine Guide*, can you find what magazine is abbreviated (*Pen Pow*)? That's (P-e-n P-o-w). (*Pause*) If you discovered that (*Pen Pow*) is the abbreviation for (*Penny Power*), you really are catching on!

CAMPING

Make-It-Yourself Camping Lantern

E.Adams.   Child D   31:33
                (Color blue)
Aug-Sep '81

FIG. 30.   Index entry that shows abbreviated magazine title

Copyright © 1981 *Children's Magazine Guide* 34(1):6 (Sept. 1981). Reprinted by permission of the publisher.

BUBBLE GUM

Bubble Gum Goes to School.

Pen Pow   2:2-5   Aug-Sep '81
(Color blue)

FIG. 31.   Another abbreviated magazine title

Copyright © 1981 *Children's Magazine Guide* 34(1):5 (Sept. 1981). Reprinted by permission of the publisher.

Our (library/media center) cannot take all of the magazines included in *Children's Magazine Guide*. I have marked the titles we take with a check mark in the boxes in front of the titles.

The magazines included in *Children's Magazine Guide* will not always be the same. Magazines that have been printed for years may not be published anymore and new magazines are always starting. The people who publish *Chil-*

*dren's Magazine Guide* keep it up to date so that you will find the magazines that our school may take.

Turn back to page 2 in your booklet, again. Turn *back* to page 2. (*Pause*) Not only magazine titles are abbreviated. To save space, other words that are used often are shortened also. The words abbreviated in *Children's Magazine Guide* are listed in the section labeled "Abbreviations." It is colored green. An example of one of these abbreviations is c-o-n-t. It is colored orange. If you see the abbreviation c-o-n-t. when you are using the index, it means that the article you want is continued in another issue of the magazine besides the one listed. Some of the abbreviations used are not letters. Some are symbols. A plus sign means that an article or story is continued somewhere else in the magazine in addition to the pages listed, usually in the back of the magazine.

What does the abbreviation of three dots mean? (*Pause*) Yes, three dots shows that some words have been left out. You will find three dots used in long titles to save space.

All abbreviations are given on the inside of the front cover of each issue of *Children's Magazine Guide*. Whenever you find an abbreviation that you can't figure out, always check this page.

Keep your copy of *Children's Magazine Guide* open to this inside cover page. Turn to page 5 (fig. 32) in your booklet. Skip pages 3 and 4 since we have already talked about them. (*Pause*) You should be looking at page 5 in your booklet now. Here is a sample of an entry you might find in *Children's Magazine Guide*.

The articles and stories included in *Children's Magazine Guide* are listed by subject only. When you learned to use the card catalog you discovered that books can be found by looking for the author, the title, or the subject. When you need magazine articles, however, you usually don't know the name of an author or the title of a magazine article. You are looking for information on a special subject. Because of this, all information listed in *Children's Magazine Guide* is given under the subject heading only.

Since all information in the *Guide* is found under the subject heading, you begin by looking for the subject in which you are interested. The subject here is (DINOSAURS). The subject heading has been colored yellow to help you find it. Notice that the subject heading is written entirely in capital letters.

Next, colored pink, is the title of an article

DINOSAURS
*(Color yellow)*

Watch Out for Dinosaurs!
*(Color pink)*

L. Pringle.   Ranger Rick
*(Color brown)   (Color green)        (Color blue)*

*(Color red)* 15:30-32   Sep '81 *(Color orange)*

FIG. 32.   Identifying the elements in an index entry

about (dinosaurs). This article has the title ("Watch Out for Dinosaurs!" [pronounce the exclamation point]). The title gives you a hint about the content of the article. Sometimes you can decide whether you want to read the entire article just by seeing the title.

After the title, and colored green, is the name of the person who wrote the article. The author of ("Watch Out for Dinosaurs!") is (L. Pringle).

The next fact you need to know is the title of the magazine that printed the article. The magazine title is colored blue. This article is in (*Ranger Rick*). The title of the magazine is abbreviated. To find what magazine is abbreviated (*Ranger Rick*), you need to look at the list of abbreviations on the inside cover page of *Children's Magazine Guide*. Look at that page in your copy of *Children's Magazine Guide* and see if you can find what (*Ranger Rick*) is short for. (*Pause*) By looking at the "Abbreviations of Magazines Indexed," you should have found that (*Ranger Rick*) is short for (*Ranger Rick's Nature Magazine*).

The number, (15), is colored red. This tells you the volume number of the magazine. Some libraries put magazines into book form and the volume tells you the book number. After the volume number, there is a colon. A colon is two dots, one above the other. The number after the colon is the page number. It is colored brown. This article will be found on pages (30 to 32).

Next, in orange, is the date of the issue of (*Ranger Rick's Nature Magazine*) that this article is in. The date given is (S-e-p apostrophe 81). (S-e-p) is short for the month of (September). The (apostrophe 81) tells you what year the article was printed. An apostrophe mark shows you that the 19 hundred of (1981) has been omitted or left out. ("Watch Out for Dino-

saurs!") can be found in the (September 1981) issue of (*Ranger Rick's Nature Magazine*).

You know the name of the magazine: (*Ranger Rick's Nature Magazine*). You know the date of the magazine: (September 1981). You know on what page the article will be found (page 30). When you turn to page (30), you will find the article, ("Watch Out for Dinosaurs!") by (L. Pringle). This is all the information you will need to find this article.

*OPTION 1: Comparison of index entry with article*

Our copy of the (September 1981) issue of (*Ranger Rick's Nature Magazine*) is on the table in front of you. Turn to page (30). (*Pause*) This is the beginning of the article about (DINOSAURS) which you found by using *Children's Magazine Guide*. If you would like to look at this article and compare the information given in *Children's Magazine Guide*, stop the tape until you are ready to continue. (*Tone*)
[End of Option 1]

Now turn to page 6 (fig. 33) in your booklet. (*Pause*) Here is another example of an article indexed in *Children's Magazine Guide*. What is the first subject heading? (*Pause*) If you said (SEA TURTLES), you are right. What is the title of the first article listed under this subject heading? (*Pause*) Yes, ("Birth of a Sea Turtle") is the name of one article about (SEA TURTLES). Can you find the author's name? (*Pause*) (W. L. Hill) is the author of this article. What is the name of the magazine where you will find this story? (*Pause*) Look at the inside cover page of your copy of *Children's Magazine Guide* again to find what the abbreviation stands for. (*Pause*) Did you discover that this article is in

(*Highlights for Children*)? If you did, you are doing very well indeed! What is the volume number of this magazine? (*Pause*) The volume is number (36). On what pages will you find this article? (*Pause*) This article will be on pages (24 and 25). What is the date of this (*Highlights for Children*)? (*Pause*) This article is in the (August/September 1981) copy of (*Highlights for Children*).

SEA TURTLES

    Birth of a Sea Turtle.  W.L.Hill.

    Highlights  36:24-25  Aug-Sep '81

    Sea Turtles in Trouble: a Plan to

    Save the Ridleys.  N.K.Williams.

    Contact  p22-25  Sep '81

SECRET CODES

FIG. 33.  Index entry with more than one reference

This page of your booklet, page 6, shows (two) different articles about (SEA TURTLES). I have drawn a line to show you how you can tell where each new index entry begins. What is the title of the second article about (SEA TURTLES)? The second article listed is ("Sea Turtles in Trouble: A Plan to Save the Ridleys").

A subject heading may have only one entry under it or there can be a long list of articles or stories on that subject. You may not find every subject in every issue of *Children's Magazine Guide*. For example, you probably will not find the subject (SEA TURTLES) in every issue.

Sometimes the subject heading may include a subheading. Page 7 (fig. 34) shows you an example. Turn to page 7 in your booklet. (*Pause*) If you look in *Children's Magazine Guide*, you may find all of these subject headings for (ART). First, there is a subject heading labeled (ART). Next, comes a subject heading that tells you about (a specific kind of ART). (Chinese art) is listed as (ART, CHINESE). Other sub-ject headings on this same subject are (ART—EXHIBITIONS; ART—STUDY AND TEACHING; and ART—THEMES). Check all of these headings if you are interested in articles about (ART).

ART

ART, CHINESE

ART - EXHIBITIONS

ART - STUDY AND TEACHING

ART - THEMES

FIG. 34.  Index entry with subheads that identify related subject entries

Sometimes when you look for a subject in *Children's Magazine Guide*, you will see something that looks like what is shown on page 8 (fig. 35) of your booklet. Turn to page 8 in your booklet. (*Pause*) If you want an article on the (BIG DIPPER), you won't find any articles listed under this subject heading. *Children's Magazine Guide* does not use the subject (BIG DIPPER). It is listed here to tell you that by looking for a different subject heading you will find an article about (the Big Dipper). This is called a "see" reference. If you "see" the subject heading (CONSTELLATIONS), you will find any articles or stories about (the Big Dipper) listed there.

Turn to page 9 (fig. 36) in your booklet. (*Pause*) Sometimes you can find articles on the subject you want under more than one subject heading. Here the subject is (GAMES). After the subject heading are the words, "see also" (Sports; Video Games). This means that there are articles and/or stories listed under the subject heading (GAMES), but you may find more information if you also look under the subject headings (SPORTS and VIDEO GAMES).

Turn to page 10 (fig. 37) in your booklet. Here is an entire page taken from *Children's Magazine Guide*. Take a few minutes and find subjects, titles of articles, names of authors, magazine titles, volumes, pages, and dates. When you

BIG DIPPER: see Constellations

CONSTELLATIONS

The Thoroughly Magnificent Richard and Robert Show. (Using the Big Dipper to Tell Time) E. Barnatowicz. Odyssey 3:20-21 Sep '81

FIG. 35. Index "see" entry

turn the tape on again, I will ask you some questions about this page. (*Tone*)

Let's see how well you have learned to use *Children's Magazine Guide*. What is the title of an article on the subject (METEORS)? (*Pause*) That's (METEORS: M-E-T-E-O-R-S). (*Pause*) Did you find the title ("Catch a Falling Star")?

How many articles are listed on that page for the subject of (MAGIC TRICKS)? (*Pause*) That's (MAGIC TRICKS). (*Pause*) There are (two) articles listed for the subject (MAGIC TRICKS).

Look for the subject (MOVIE ACTORS AND ACTRESSES). (*Pause*) (MOVIE ACTORS AND ACTRESSES) is the subject you are looking for. (*Pause*) Why aren't there any articles listed under this subject? (*Pause*) Did you remember that sometimes you have to look under a different subject heading to find the information you want? What subject should you see to find information on (MOVIE ACTORS AND ACTRESSES)? (*Pause*) Yes, you would look for the subject heading (ACTORS AND ACTRESSES).

What other subject heading can you look under to find more articles with information on (MONEY)? (*Pause*) If you said you would look under the subject (SILVER) for more articles about (MONEY), you are doing a really super job with this.

GAMES: see also Sports; Video Games

Changing the Rules. B.B.Mackey. Highlights 36:34-35 Aug-Sep '81

Famous Fast Finger Flicker. Chickadee 3:15-18 Sep '81

SPORTS

Walking, Jogging, or Running-- Which is Best for You? B. Weinstein. Sci World 38:21-23 Sep 4 '81

VIDEO GAMES

The Real Story Behind Space Invaders? H.J.Blumenthal. Sci World 38:8-10 Sep 18 '81

FIG. 36. Index "see also" entry

Now, put down your booklet and pick up your copy of *Children's Magazine Guide*. See if you can find articles and stories about (VOLCANOES). All subject headings are in alphabetical order. When you find the page with the subject heading (VOLCANOES), start the tape again. (*Tone*)

If you were able to find the subject heading (VOLCANOES), on page (*specify*), you know how to locate subjects in *Children's Magazine Guide*. If you feel that you understand the information that is included in an entry, you

15

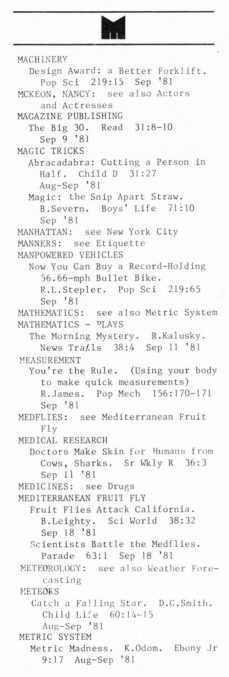

MACHINERY
    Design Award: a Better Forklift.
    Pop Sci  219:15  Sep '81
MCKEON, NANCY:  see also Actors
    and Actresses
MAGAZINE PUBLISHING
    The Big 30.  Read  31:8-10
    Sep 9 '81
MAGIC TRICKS
    Abracadabra: Cutting a Person in
    Half.  Child D  31:27
    Aug-Sep '81
    Magic: the Snip Apart Straw.
    B.Severn.  Boys' Life  71:10
    Sep '81
MANHATTAN:  see New York City
MANNERS:  see Etiquette
MANPOWERED VEHICLES
    Now You Can Buy a Record-Holding
    56.66-mph Bullet Bike.
    R.L.Stepler.  Pop Sci  219:65
    Sep '81
MATHEMATICS:  see also Metric System
MATHEMATICS - PLAYS
    The Morning Mystery.  R.Kalusky.
    News Trails  38:4  Sep 11 '81
MEASUREMENT
    You're the Rule.  (Using your body
    to make quick measurements)
    R.James.  Pop Mech  156:170-171
    Sep '81
MEDFLIES:  see Mediterranean Fruit
    Fly
MEDICAL RESEARCH
    Doctors Make Skin for Humans from
    Cows, Sharks.  Sr Wkly R  36:3
    Sep 11 '81
MEDICINES:  see Drugs
MEDITERRANEAN FRUIT FLY
    Fruit Flies Attack California.
    B.Leighty.  Sci World  38:32
    Sep 18 '81
    Scientists Battle the Medflies.
    Parade  63:1  Sep 18 '81
METEOROLOGY:  see also Weather Fore-
    casting
METEORS
    Catch a Falling Star.  D.G.Smith.
    Child Life  60:14-15
    Aug-Sep '81
METRIC SYSTEM
    Metric Madness.  K.Odom.  Ebony Jr
    9:17  Aug-Sep '81

MICE - STORIES
    Little Red.  E.Ward.  Chickadee
    3:20-23  Sep '81
MIDDLE EAST
    The Middle East--1981.  (News
    map)  Jr Schol  84:8-9
    Sep 4 '81
    The Middle East: Sitting on a
    Powderkeg.  Jr Schol  84:7+
    Sep 4 '81
MIGRATION, INTERNAL:  see Population
MILITARY AIRPLANES:  see Airplanes,
    Military
MILK:  see also Cheese
MINIMUM WAGE
    Are Teens Willing to Work for
    Less Than Minimum Wage?
    D.Pawelek.  Sr Schol  114:6+
    Sep 4 '81
MODEL AIRPLANES:  see also Paper
    Airplanes
MONA LISA:  see DaVinci, Leonardo
MONEY:  see also Silver
    Money.  Sprint  7:12-13
    Sep 18 '81
    Money, Money, Money.  P.M.Jones.
    Sr Schol  114:14-16  Sep 4 '81
MOTION PICTURES:  see Movies
MOTORBOATS
    The Wettest, Wildest Outboard.
    B.McKeown.  Pop Mech  156:99
    Sep '81
MOTORCYCLES AND MOTORCYCLING
    How to Stretch Your Riding Season.
    B.Hampton.  Pop Mech  156:198+
    Sep '81
    Pocketbikes: Little Bikes, Big
    Problems?  Extra  15:2
    Sep 16 '81
MOVIE ACTORS AND ACTRESSES:  see
    Actors and Actresses
MOVIE REVIEWS
    At the Movies.  (Superman II;
    The Eye of the Needle; The Fan)
    L.Konner & P.Fisher.  Young Miss
    29:23  Sep '81
    Honky Tonk Freeway.  M.Ronan.
    Sci World  38:26  Sep 4 '81;
    Search  14:26  Sep 4 '81;
    Sr Schol  114:26  Sep 4 '81
MOVIES
    Super Heroes of the Silver Screen.
    C.B.Roman.  Co-ed  27:25
    Sep '81
    Superman II: Has Superman Turned
    Super Human?  M.Ronan.  Dyn
    5:10-11  Sep '81
MUSEUMS:  see also Children's Mu-
    seums; Sports Museums

FIG. 37.  Sample page of index entries

should be ready to try the worksheet I will give to you. If you are uncertain about how to use *Children's Magazine Guide*, play through the tape again. You can also go over the booklet again and review your copy of *Children's Magazine Guide.*

When you feel confident that you can use *Children's Magazine Guide* to find articles and stories in magazines, you are ready for the quiz. Good luck!

[End of Script]

*WORKSHEET*

```
          MYSTERY AND DETECTIVE PLAYS
            Menace in the Mist.  D.Kerr
           Child D  31:38-42  Aug-Sep '81
```

1.  Identify all the parts of the index entry above:

    a.  Magazine title  _____

    b.  Article title  _____

    c.  Page number  _____

    d.  Subject heading  _____

    e.  Date of magazine  _____

    f.  Author  _____

    g.  Volume  _____

2.  What does the abbreviation "concl." mean?  _____

3.  What is the full title of the magazine that is abbreviated

    "Playmate"?  _____

4.  Using the copy of Children's Magazine Guide in front of you, choose

    a subject that interests you.  Write down all of the information

    you need to find an article or story on that subject.  Locate the

    magazine that the article is in and bring it to me with this paper.

        SUBJECT:  _____

        Article Information:  _____

                              _____

                              _____

                              _____

# 6 ABRIDGED READERS' GUIDE TO PERIODICAL LITERATURE

Although the *Abridged Readers' Guide to Periodical Literature* is not found in most elementary school library media centers, students in the fifth and sixth grades should be introduced to it so that they can become familiar with this useful tool. Students will need to use this reference tool in the secondary schools and in the public library. When mastery of this index is complete, the skill is transferrable to many other indexes.

In this kit, the student will be introduced to the rationale for using a periodical index and become familiar with the physical arrangement of the *Abridged Readers' Guide to Periodical Literature*, especially the front pages which contain basic information. The student will analyze an entry in depth and discover the elements of an index entry. The student will also become familiar with "See," "See Also," and Book Review entries.

## Materials Needed:

1 Issue of the *Abridged Readers' Guide to Periodical Literature*
9 Colored pencils (yellow, blue, red, orange, green, dark green, pink, purple and brown)
1 Felt-tip pen (black)
1 Two- or three-ring notebook binder
1 Blank cassette tape

1 Mimeo or ditto master
1 Periodical to correspond to figure 42 (optional).

## Preparing the Visual Book:

1. Use a copy machine to transfer the following pages from the *Abridged Readers' Guide to Periodical Literature*:
   a. Cover (*see* fig. 38):
      1) Draw a circle around the title with black felt-tip pen.
      2) Color the date blue.
      3) Color the volume and number yellow.
      4) Color the indexing dates pink.
      5) Color "The H. W. Wilson Company" green.
   b. "Abbreviations of Publications Indexed" (*see* fig. 39):
      1) Color "Abbreviations of Publications Indexed" pink.
      2) Color one periodical abbreviation blue (Sample used: *Am Heritage*).
      3) Draw a circle around the explanation of materials for the blind.
   c. "Abbreviations" (*see* fig. 40):
      1) Color "Abbreviations" red.
      2) Color the "+" abbreviation blue.
   d. "Periodicals Indexed" (*see* fig. 41):
      1) Color "Periodicals Indexed" red.

2) Color the periodical title blue (Sample used: *American Heritage*).
3) Color the price yellow.
4) Color the frequency of publication green.
5) Color the address brown.
2. Trim pages and mount on 8½″ x 11″ paper.
3. Type the following:
   a. Complete subject entry (*see* fig. 42):
      1) Color subject heading blue.
      2) Color title yellow.
      3) Color description green (optional).
      4) Color author's name orange.
      5) Color "il" and/or "por" pink.
      6) Color periodical abbreviation brown.
      7) Color volume number purple.
      8) Color page numbers red.
      9) Underline date of publication dark green.
   b. Complete subject entry with subheading (*see* fig. 43):
      1) Color subheading yellow.
   c. "See" reference with complete entry under "see" subject (*see* fig. 44).
   d. "See also" reference with complete entry under "see also" subject (*see* fig. 45):
      1) Draw a line from "see also" reference to the "see also" subject heading.
   e. Book review entry (*see* fig. 46):
      1) Color the author's name green.
      2) Color the title of the book red.
      3) Color the periodical title blue.
      4) Color the volume number yellow.
      5) Color the page numbers brown.
      6) Color the date purple.
      7) Color the reviewer's name orange.
4. Laminate the pages or insert into plastic protective sheaths for durability.
5. Punch two or three holes in each page.
6. Put illustrations (figs. 38–46) into notebook binder in proper sequence indicated by numerical order.

# Preparing the Script:

1. Read the script, select, and/or substitute the terminology congruent with that used in your library/media center.

2. Choose Option 1A or 1B.
3. Decide if you wish to use Option 2.
4. Make changes in the script so that references are for your samples.
5. Proofread the script to correct any oversights or errors.
6. Record the script onto the blank cassette tape.

# Preparing the Worksheet:

1. Type the worksheet as written
                    or
2. Substitute other examples.

# Preparing for Student Use:

1. Arrange a table and chair near the *Abridged Readers' Guide to Periodical Literature*, if possible.
2. Insert the recorded tape cassette into a cassette player with earphones.
3. Place a copy of the *Abridged Readers' Guide to Periodical Literature* on the table.
4. Put a copy of the periodical used in figure 42 on the table (Option 2).
5. Give the student the visual book.

# Script

*OPTION 1A: No previous index experience*
   You have learned how to find books by using the card catalog. Sometimes, however, you will not be able to find the information you need in a book because your subject will be too new to be in a book. It takes a long time to write and publish a book and even longer until the book is

here in our (library/media center), ready for your use. When you want up-to-date facts and information, you will need to look for magazine articles. Magazine articles also can be used to add to the information you find in books. Magazines have articles and stories on a wide number of subjects.

To find magazine articles, you need special help. You could take all of the magazines which we have at (*name of school*) and look for articles about your subject. That would waste a lot of your time and you probably would not find what you need. To find a book, you learned to look in the card catalog. To find the magazine article you need, you should look in an index to magazine articles. The index which we use in our (library/media center) is the *Abridged Readers' Guide to Periodical Literature.*

*OPTION 1B: Previous index experience with* Children's Magazine Guide

You have learned to use *Children's Magazine Guide* to find articles in magazines. When you go on to (junior high/middle/intermediate) school or the public library, you will find another index, the *Abridged Readers' Guide to Periodical Literature.* Today you will learn to use this index.

[End of Option 1]

On the table in front of you is a copy of the *Abridged Readers' Guide to Periodical Literature.* There is also a copy of the booklet you will be using. Open your booklet to page 1 (fig. 38). Page 1 of your booklet is a copy of the cover of the *Abridged Readers' Guide to Periodical Literature.* Look at the title. In your booklet, it has a black circle drawn around it.

The title of this index may sound strange to you, but it isn't as difficult as it seems at first. The first word, "Abridged," means shortened. This index is a shortened version of the *Readers' Guide to Periodical Literature* which is found in (the public library and/or in the high school [library/media center]). Because this index is abridged, there are not as many magazines listed as you would find in the *Readers' Guide to Periodical Literature.* The magazines that are included in the *Abridged Readers' Guide to Periodical Literature* are the magazines most likely to be found in (elementary and [junior high/middle/intermediate]) schools. There are thousands of periodicals printed, but these are the ones that are most widely read by students.

The next two words of the title are used together. "Readers' Guide" means that the index helps people who read and use magazines. The guide will lead readers to the information they want.

The last two words of the title, "Periodical Literature" could be changed to the word "magazines." Something that is published on a regular schedule, such as once a month, once a week, or every day, is called a periodical. "Literature" is something which is printed so that people can read it. What all of this says is that the *Abridged Readers' Guide to Periodical Literature* is an index to magazines, just as the card catalog is an index to books.

Now look at the top of the cover. The date of this issue of the *Abridged Readers' Guide to Periodical Literature* is colored blue to help you find it on this sample. The date is (May 1981). This is the date this issue of the *Abridged Readers' Guide to Periodical Literature* was published. The *Abridged Readers' Guide to Periodical Literature* is printed each month of the school year. It is not published in June, July, or August. Three times a year—in May, September, and January—the issues are combined so that you do not have to look in so many different books when you are hunting for magazine articles. Once a year, in February, all of the indexes for the past year are combined into one book.

Look at the information that is colored yellow. It is just below the month and year. This is the volume and number of the issue. This volume of the *Abridged Readers' Guide to Periodical Literature* is number (47) and the number is (3).

Next, in pink, under the volume and number, are the dates of the magazines that are included in this issue of the *Abridged Readers' Guide to Periodical Literature.* The periodicals included for indexing in this issue have dates from (January 28 to April 21, 1981. This is an issue that includes articles published in January, February, March, and April.)

At the bottom of the cover page, in the area colored green, is the name of the company which publishes the index, The H. W. Wilson Company.

Turn to page 2 (fig. 39) of your booklet. (*Pause*) The title of this page, "Abbreviations of Publications Indexed," is colored red. Now find this same page in the copy of the *Abridged Readers' Guide to Periodical Literature* on the table in

**This is a quarterly cumulative issue. No further reference to March No. 1, and April No. 2 is necessary.**

**MAY 1981**
*(Color blue)*

**Vol. 47   No. 3**
*(Color yellow)*

Includes indexing from January 28—April 21, 1981
*(Color pink)*

# ABRIDGED
# READERS' GUIDE
## to periodical literature

An author subject index

to periodicals commonly

used for reference in

public and school libraries.

**THE H. W. WILSON COMPANY**
*(Color green)*

**ISSN 0001-334X**

FIG. 38.   Cover of May 1981 issue

# ABBREVIATIONS OF PUBLICATIONS INDEXED —*(Color pink)*

### For full information, consult pages v-vi

*Am Heritage–American Heritage   *(Color blue)*
Am Hist Illus–American History Illustrated
Art News–Art News
*Atlantic–Atlantic

*Bet Hom & Gard–Better Homes and Gardens
Bus W–Business Week

*Changing T–Changing Times
Cong Digest–Congressional Digest
Creat Crafts–Creative Crafts
Cur Hist–Current History

*Ebony–Ebony
Educ Digest–Education Digest
Environment–Environment

*Fam Health–Family Health incorporating To-day's Health
*50 Plus–50 Plus
*For Aff–Foreign Affairs

*Good H–Good Housekeeping

*Harpers–Harper's
Hi Fi–High Fidelity and Musical America
*Horizon–Horizon

*Money–Money
Motor T–Motor Trend
*Ms–Ms.

N Y Times Bk R–New York Times Book Review
N Y Times Mag–New York Times Magazine
*Nat Geog–National Geographic Magazine
*Nat Geog World–National Geographic World
*Nat R–National Review (48p issue only, pub. in alternate weeks)
Nat Wildlife–National Wildlife
*Natur Hist–Natural History
Negro Hist Bull–Negro History Bulletin

New Repub–New Republic
New Yorker–New Yorker
*Newsweek–Newsweek

*Outdoor Life–Outdoor Life (Northeast edition)

*Parents–Parents
People–People Weekly
Peter Phot Mag–Petersen's Photographic Magazine
Pop Electr–Popular Electronics
*Pop Mech–Popular Mechanics
Pop Sci–Popular Science
*Psychol Today–Psychology Today

Read Digest–Reader's Digest
Roll Stone–Rolling Stone

Sat Eve Post–Saturday Evening Post
*Sat R–Saturday Review
*Sci Am–Scientific American
Sci Digest–Science Digest
*Sci News–Science News
*Seventeen–Seventeen
*Smithsonian–Smithsonian
Society–Society
*Sports Illus–Sports Illustrated
Sr Schol–Senior Scholastic including World Week (Scholastic Teacher's edition)
Suc Farm–Successful Farming (Midwest edition)

Time–Time
Todays Educ–Today's Education (General edition)

*U.S. News–U.S. News & World Report

World Week. See Senior Scholastic

* Available for blind and other physically handicapped readers on talking books, in braille, or on magnetic tape. For information address Division for the Blind and Physically Handicapped Library of Congress, Washington, D.C. 20542

Abr G 5/81

Fɪɢ. 39.  Abbreviations for indexed publications

front of you. When you find the page, compare it to the one in your sample book. (*Pause*) This page shows a list of the periodical abbreviations used in the *Abridged Readers' Guide to Periodical Literature*. Abbreviations are shortened words. Abbreviations are used whenever possible to keep the *Abridged Readers' Guide* from having too many pages.

Look at the first magazine listed on this page. It is colored blue in the sample. Instead of (*American Heritage*) written out completely, you will find only (*Am Heritage*) in an entry in the *Abridged Readers' Guide to Periodical Literature*. If you do not know what magazine (*Am Heritage*) is when you see it in an entry, turn to this page and you can find its full title.

What periodical is abbreviated (C-u-r H-i-s-t)? (*Pause*) Did you look through the abbreviations and find that this abbreviation stands for (*Current History*)? Let's try one more. What magazine is listed as (*S-a-t R*)? (*Pause*) Yes, (*Sat R*) is the abbreviation for (*Saturday Review*).

Notice that some of the titles have a star in front of them. The star is explained at the bottom of the page. I have drawn a circle around the explanation on your sample. The magazines marked with a star can be bought in braille or on tapes for people who are blind.

At (*name of your school*), we do not have all of the periodicals that are indexed in the *Abridged Readers' Guide to Periodical Literature*. To see if we take the magazine here at (*name of school*), I have marked your copy of the *Abridged Readers' Guide to Periodical Literature* (*describe how you have marked your periodical list*). These are the periodicals you can find in our magazine section. You will find our magazines (*describe the location*). The periodicals we take at (*name of school*) are (*read the titles*).

We keep our back issues of periodicals for (*number of years*) years. The back issues can be found (*describe the location*).

You are ready to go on to page 3 (fig. 40) in your booklet. (*Pause*). This page is called "Abbreviations." I have colored the title red. Find the same page in your copy of the *Abridged Readers' Guide to Periodical Literature*. (*Pause*) This page lists some other abbreviations used in the *Abridged Readers' Guide*. You just learned that magazine titles are abbreviated, or shortened, whenever possible to save space in the index. To keep the index from being too big,

words that are used often also are abbreviated. All of the abbreviations used in the *Abridged Readers' Guide to Periodical Literature* are shown on this page.

Some abbreviations are symbols instead of letters. Look at the abbreviation colored blue. A plus sign means that an article is continued beyond the pages listed in the index entry.

If you find an abbreviation used in an entry in the *Abridged Readers' Guide to Periodical Literature* that you do not understand, simply turn to this page in the front of the index. Now, take a few minutes and look at these abbreviations. Stop the tape until you are ready to continue. (*Tone*)

Did you notice that each month has its own abbreviation? Even May, which is only three letters long when it is spelled out, is abbreviated M-y. January, June, and July are all months that begin with J, but they are also abbreviated with two letters. Some months, such as October and December, are shortened to one letter. What does an (F) stand for? (*Pause*) Did you discover that (F) is the abbreviation for (February)? What is abbreviated (by a small v)? (*Pause*) Yes, (the small v) is short for (volume).

Turn to page 4 (fig. 41) in your booklet. (*Pause*) This sample page from the *Abridged Readers' Guide to Periodical Literature* is labeled "Periodicals Indexed." The title has been colored red to help you find it. Now find this same page in your copy of the *Abridged Readers' Guide to Periodical Literature*. (*Pause*) The "Periodicals Indexed" section gives the address and price of each magazine indexed in the *Abridged Readers' Guide*. Look at the magazine title that has been colored blue. The title of this magazine is (*American Heritage*). The price of (*American Heritage*) is colored yellow. It costs ($21.00) for a one-year subscription. Next, colored green, is an abbreviation (bi-m). To find what it means you would look on the page of abbreviations for (bi-dash-m). You would find that (bi dash m) means (bi-monthly). (Bi-monthly) means that the magazine is published (every other month or six times a year). Last, and colored brown, is the address to which you can write if you want to subscribe to the magazine for yourself.

Can you find the listing for (*National Geographic World*) on this same page? (*Pause*) How much would a subscription to (*National Geographic World*) cost, if you wanted to order it? (*Pause*) Yes, the price is ($6.95) for a one-year

# ABBREVIATIONS
*(Color red)*

| | | | |
|---|---|---|---|
| * | following name entry, a printer's device | Jl | July |
| | | Jr | Junior |
| + | continued on later pages of same issue | jt auth | joint author |
| Abp | Archbishop   *(Color blue)* | Ltd | Limited |
| abr | abridged | | |
| Ag | August | m | monthly |
| Ap | April | Mr | March |
| arch | architect | My | May |
| Assn | Association | | |
| Aut | Autumn | N | November |
| Ave | Avenue | no | number |
| | | | |
| Bart | Baronet | O | October |
| bibl | bibliography | | |
| bibl f | bibliographical footnotes | por | portrait |
| bi-m | bimonthly | pseud | pseudonym |
| bi-w | biweekly | pt | part |
| bldg | building | pub | published, publisher, publishing |
| Bp | Bishop | | |
| Co | Company | q | quarterly |
| comp | compiled, compiler | | |
| cond | condensed | rev | revised |
| cont | continued | | |
| Corp | Corporation | S | September |
| | | sec | section |
| D | December | semi-m | semimonthly |
| Dept | Department | Soc | Society |
| | | Spr | Spring |
| ed | edited, edition, editor | Sq | Square |
| | | Sr | Senior |
| | | St | Street |
| F | February | Summ | Summer |
| | | supp | supplement |
| | | supt | superintendent |
| Hon | Honorable | | |
| | | tr | translated, translation, translator |
| il | illustrated, illustration, illustrator | | |
| Inc | Incorporated | v | volume |
| int | interviewer | | |
| introd | introduction, introductory | w | weekly |
| | | Wint | Winter |
| Ja | January | | |
| Je | June | yr | year |

FIG. 40.  Abbreviations for other words used in entries

## PERIODICALS INDEXED

*(Color red)*

**All data as of latest issue received**

*(Color blue)    (Color yellow)  (Color green)        (Color brown)*

\*American Heritage–$21. bi-m American Heritage, 205 W Center St, Marion, Ohio 43302

American History Illustrated–$15. m (except Mr, S) The National Historical Society, 3300 Walnut St, Boulder, Colo. 80302

Art News–$20. m (q Je-Ag) Art News, P.O. Box 969, Farmingdale, N.Y. 11737

\*The Atlantic–18. m Atlantic, P.O. Box 1857, Greenwich, Conn. 06830

\*Better Homes and Gardens–$12. m Better Homes and Gardens, 1716 Locust St, Des Moines, Ia. 50336

Business Week–$34.95. w (except for one issue in Ja) Business Week, P.O. Box 430, Hightstown, N.J. 08520

\*Changing Times–$12. m Changing Times, The Kiplinger Magazine, Editors Park, Md. 20782

Congressional Digest–$20. m (bi-m Je-Jl, Ag-S) Congressional Digest Corp, 3231 P St, NW, Washington, D.C. 20007

Creative Crafts–$7. bi-m Circulation Manager, Creative Crafts, P.O. Box 700, Newton, N.J. 07860

Current History–$18.85. m (except Je, Jl, Ag) Current History, Inc, 4225 Main St, Philadelphia, Pa. 19127

\*Ebony–$12. m Ebony, 820 S Michigan Ave, Chicago, Ill. 60605

The Education Digest–$12. m (S-My) Prakken Publications, Inc, 416 Longshore Drive, Ann Arbor, Mich. 48107

Environment–$25. m (bi-m Ja-F, Jl-Ag) Environment, 4000 Albemarle St, NW, Washington, D.C. 20016

\*Family Health incorporating Todays Health–$15. m (bi-m Jl-Ag, N-D) Family Health, P.O. Box 3700, Bergenfield, N.J. 07621

\*50 Plus–$12.50. m 50 Plus, 99 Garden St, Marion, Ohio 43302

\*Foreign Affairs–$18. 5 times a year Foreign Affairs, Subscription Dept, P.O. Box 2615, Boulder, Colo. 80321

\*Good Housekeeping–$9.97. m Good Housekeeping, P.O. Box 10055, Des Moines, Ia. 50350

\*Harper's–$14. m Harper's, 1255 Portland Pl, Boulder, Colo. 80303

High Fidelity and Musical America–$24. m High Fidelity, 1 Sound Ave, Marion, Ohio 43302

\*Horizon–$18. m Horizon, 381 W Center St, Marion, Ohio 43302

\*Money–$19.95. m Money, Time-Life Bldg, 541 N Fairbanks Court, Chicago, Ill. 60611

Motor Trend–$11.94. m Motor Trend, P.O. Box 3290, Los Angeles, Calif. 90028

\*Ms.–$10. m Ms. Magazine, 123 Garden St, Marion, Ohio 43302

Musical America. See High Fidelity and Musical America

\*National Geographic Magazine–$11. m The Secretary, National Geographic Society, Washington, D.C. 20036

\*National Geographic World–$6.95. m National Geographic World, 17th and M Sts, NW, Washington, D.C. 20036

\*National Review–$24. bi-w (48p issue) National Review, 150 E 35th St, New York, N.Y. 10016

National Wildlife–$9.50. bi-m National Wildlife Federation, 1412 16th St, NW, Washington, D.C. 20036

\*Natural History–$15. m (bi-m Je-Jl, Ag-S) Natural History, Membership Services, Box 4300, Bergenfield, N.J. 07621

The Negro History Bulletin–$16. 4 times a year Association for the Study of Negro Life and History, Inc, 1401 14th St, NW, Washington, D.C. 20005

The New Republic–$28. w (48 issues a yr) New Republic, P.O. Box 955, Farmingdale, N.Y. 11737

New York Times Book Review–$18. w The New York Times Co, Times Sq, New York, N.Y. 10036

The New York Times Magazine–$77.75. w (complete Sunday ed; not sold separately) New York Times, Times Bldg, 229 W 43rd St, New York, N.Y. 10036

The New Yorker–$28. w New Yorker Magazine, Inc, 25 W 43rd St, New York, N.Y. 10036

\*Newsweek–$32.50. w Newsweek, The Newsweek Building, Livingston, N.J. 07039

\*Outdoor Life (Northeast edition)–$11.94. m Outdoor Life, Boulder, Colo. 80302

\*Parents'–$9.95. m Parents' Magazine, Bergenfield, N.J. 07621

Abr G 5/81

FIG. 41.  Identifying the elements of an index entry

subscription to this periodical. How often is (*National Geographic World*) published? (*Pause*) Did you find an (m)? Can you find what (m) is the abbreviation for? Look back to the page of abbreviations in your copy of the *Abridged Readers' Guide to Periodical Literature*. (*Pause*) (M) means that (*National Geographic World*) is published once a month. The address for this magazine is (*read the address*).

How much does a subscription to (*Ebony*) cost for one year? (*Pause*) A subscription to (Ebony) is ($12) for one year. Where would you write for a subscription to (*Creative Crafts*)? (*Pause*) If you said (P.O. Box 700, Newton, New Jersey 07860), you are finding information on this page just the way you should.

Now that you know how to use these pages which are located in the front of every copy of the *Abridged Readers' Guide to Periodical Literature*, you are ready to learn to use the index itself. Keep your copy of the *Abridged Readers' Guide* open. Turn to page 5 (fig. 42) in your booklet. (*Pause*) Page 5 of your booklet shows a sample of an actual entry in the *Abridged Readers' Guide to Periodical Literature*. In the card catalog, books are indexed by the author, the title, and the subject. The *Abridged Readers' Guide to Periodical Literature* lists articles by author and subject only. Titles are not included because it is not very often that people know the exact title of a magazine article they want to use. In fact, most times when you use the *Abridged Readers' Guide to Periodical Literature*, you will not look for an author's name. You will be hunting for information about a certain subject.

In this sample, the subject is (gorillas). The subject heading has been colored blue to help you find it. Notice that the subject, (GORILLAS), is written in capital letters just as subjects are written in capital letters in the card catalog.

Under the subject heading is the title of an article about (gorillas). This has been colored yellow. In this entry, the title of the article is ("Don't mess with the birthday boy: the oldest gorilla in captivity turns 50"). In brackets, after the title and colored green, is a brief description of the information in the article. ["Massa at the Philadelphia Zoo"] tells you that (the gorilla's name is Massa and he lives at the Philadelphia Zoo).

Next, in orange, is the author of this article, (M. Donovan). Notice that the author's name comes after the title of the article.

The abbreviations that come next, i-l and p-o-r, are colored pink. To find out what i-l and p-o-r stand for, you must look in the list of abbreviations in the front of your copy of the *Abridged Readers' Guide to Periodical Literature*. Turn to the page titled, "Abbreviations," and find the letters i-l. When you learn what i-l means, start the tape again. (*Tone*)

Did you discover that i-l stands for illustrated, illustration, or illustrator? This means that the article ("Don't mess with the birthday boy: the oldest gorilla in captivity turns 50") has pictures of some kind.

Now, find the abbreviation p-o-r. (*Tone*) Did you find that p-o-r is the abbreviation for portrait? A portrait is a photograph or picture of the face of a person or living thing. In this article, the portrait is probably of (Massa, the gorilla who is 50 years old).

Next, colored brown in your sample, is the name of the magazine which published the article ("Don't mess with the birthday boy: the oldest gorilla in captivity turns 50"). The abbreviation used is (*People*). To find the complete title of this magazine, turn to the list of "Abbreviations of Publications Indexed" in the front of your copy of the *Abridged Readers' Guide to Periodical Literature*. (*Tone*) Did you learn that (*People*) is short for (*People Weekly*)? (*People Weekly*) is the magazine which published the (gorilla) story indexed in this sample.

The information colored purple and red will help you find the exact issue and page of this article in (*People Weekly*). First, look at the number colored purple. This first number, (15), tells you what volume of (*People Weekly*) you want. Sometimes magazines are put into book form and this would be the number of the book, or bound volume, as it is called. You will need this volume number if your teacher asks you to write a bibliography.

After the (15) you see a colon. Colon is the name for the punctuation mark made with two dots, one above the other. The colon is followed by the numbers (57 dash 8), colored red. The numbers after the colon are the page numbers of the magazine on which you will find the article. The article about the gorilla is on pages (57 and 58). Notice that the entire page number is not given for the page where the article ends when the first part of the number is the same. If this article were on pages (57 to 62), it would be written (57 to 62) with all numbers written out completely. Since this article is on (two) pages that are numbered in the (50s), it is written (57

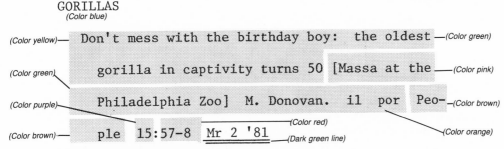

FIG. 42.   Elements of sample index entry

dash 8). The first page number, the one that indicates where the article begins, is given in full. When you see the number (57), you know that page (57) is where the article starts. The dash means that all the pages between that first number and the last number will be part of the article. The last number leaves out the (fifty) of the page number and gives only the (8). At this point, you still do not know the month and year that this article appeared in the (*People Weekly*).

Look at the information underlined in dark green. At the very end of each entry, the date of the magazine is written. In this case, the article ("Don't mess with the birthday boy: the oldest gorilla in captivity turns 50") was in the (M-r 2 apostrophe 81) issue of (*People Weekly*). To help you remember what the (M-r) stands for, turn to the page of "Abbreviations" in your copy of the *Abridged Readers' Guide to Periodical Literature* and check what (M-r) is the abbreviation for. (*Tone*)

(Mr) is short for (March). The (2) is the day of the month the magazine came out. Since (*People Weekly*) is printed every (week), the day is important. (Apostrophe 81) stands for the year the article was published. The 19 hundred part of (1981) is left out since the editors figure that you will know that the year is (1981), not (1881) or (2081).

*OPTION 2: Sample of the article just discussed*

On the table in front of you is the (March 2, 1981) issue of (*People Weekly*). Turn to page (57) in this issue of (*People Weekly*). (*Pause*) Here is the article, ("Don't mess with the birthday boy: the oldest gorilla in captivity turns 50"). Notice that the article begins on page (57) and is continued on page (58). Look at the illus-

trations and the portrait mentioned in the index. Can you find the author's name? (*Pause*) If you would like to spend some time comparing this article to the index information, stop the tape until you are ready to go on. (*Tone*)

[End of Option 2]

Let's look at another entry in the *Abridged Readers' Guide to Periodical Literature*. Turn to page 6 (fig. 43) in your booklet. Here is another subject entry. This time the subject is (VIDEOTAPES). The subject heading is printed in capital letters. Now look at what comes next under the subject heading. There is another heading—(Popular music). This has been colored yellow. The first letter of this heading is a capital letter, but the other letters are small or lowercase letters. (Popular music) is a subheading under the main subject heading, (VIDEOTAPES).

Let's see what you know about the article listed under this subheading. What is the title of the article about (VIDEOTAPES—Popular music)? (*Pause*) The title is ("Video music fact or fantasy?"). Who wrote the article? (*Pause*) The author of this article was (M. Amato). Where will you find this article? (*Pause*) Take the time to check out the "Abbreviations of Publications Indexed" in your copy of the *Abridged Readers' Guide to Periodical Literature*. (*Tone*) Did you find that (*Hi Fi*) is the abbreviation for (*High Fidelity and Musical America*)? Can you figure out the date without checking your abbreviations list? (*Pause*) This article appeared in the (February 1981) issue. What volume of (*High Fidelity and Musical America*) is this? (*Pause*) The volume number is (31).

VIDEOTAPES

**Popular music**
*(Color yellow)*

Video music fact or fantasy?  M. Amato.  il Hi Fi

   31:A10-A12+  F '81

FIG. 43.  Index entry with a subject heading and subhead

On what page does this article begin? (*Pause*) The article begins on page (A10). What other pages will you find the article continued to? (*Pause*) This article is continued on page(s) (A11 and A12). What does the plus mean after the (A12)? (*Pause*) If you have forgotten, look at your list of abbreviations. (*Tone*) Yes, the plus means that this article will be continued somewhere else in the magazine. It may be continued for only a few paragraphs or for many pages; we don't know until we look at the article. You did very well on that. Keep up the good work!

Turn to page 7 (fig. 44) in your booklet. (*Pause*) Do you remember when you were learning to use the card catalog, you discovered that the subject you were looking for was not always listed in the card catalog by that name?

This is also true in the *Abridged Readers' Guide to Periodical Literature*. Sometimes you will see an entry that looks like the one on page 7 in your booklet. This entry tells you that you must look under a different subject heading to find the subject you want. This example uses the subject (DOLLAR). If you look for (DOLLAR), you will see an entry that reads (DOLLAR. See Money). This means that although articles are not listed under the subject of (DOLLAR), you will find information about (the dollar) under the subject heading (MONEY).

Let's go on to page 8 (fig. 45) in your booklet. Sometimes there is information under one subject heading, but to find more information on that subject, you can look under other subject headings also. For instance, on page 8 in your booklet, you see that you can find additional

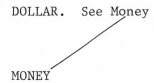

DOLLAR.  See Money

MONEY

   Buck starts here [dollar's strength]  D. Pauly

     and others.  il  Newsweek  97:59-60  F 16 '81

   Gold and the dollar in a flip-flop.  C. Byron

     and others.  il  Time  117:66  F 16 '81

   Toll of a resurgent dollar.  il  Bus W  p21-3 F16

     '81

FIG. 44.  Index "see" entry

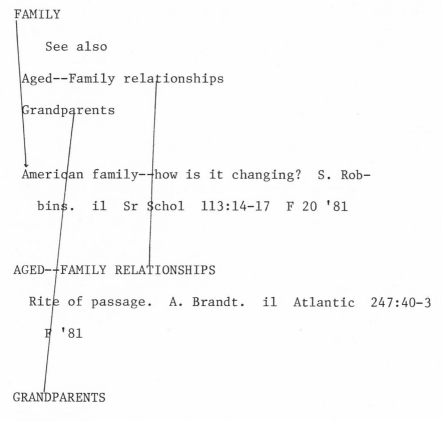

FIG. 45.    Index "see also" entry

information about (FAMILY), if you will also look for the subjects, (AGED—FAMILY RELATIONSHIPS and GRANDPARENTS).

Sometimes one volume of the *Abridged Readers' Guide to Periodical Literature* will not list the subject you want. All subjects are not covered in every issue, so you may have to look in several issues before you find entries for the subject heading you need.

There is one additional section of the *Abridged Readers' Guide* that you should know about. At the back of every issue, there is a list of book reviews which have appeared in the periodicals indexed in the *Abridged Readers' Guide to Periodical Literature*. Turn to page 9 (fig. 46) in your booklet. (*Pause*) Book reviews are listed in alphabetical order by the author of the book. The author's name is colored green in this sample. The author is (D. Taylor). The last

name is written first, followed by the initial of the author's first name. Following the author's name is the name of the book. This is colored red in your sample. The title of this book is (*Going wild: adventures of a zoo vet*).

Next, colored blue in your sample, is the name of the periodical which printed the book review. This book review was in the (*New York Times Book Review*). After this, and colored yellow, is the volume number. This is volume (86).

Following the colon and colored brown are the pages this book review is on. This review begins on page (14) and is continued (somewhere else in the magazine). Next, colored purple, is the date. This issue of the (*New York Times Book Review*) was printed (February 15, 1981). At the very end of the entry is the name of the person who wrote the book review. This is

Taylor, D.  Going wild:  adventures of a zoo vet
     *(Color green)*                    *(Color red)*

N Y Times Bk R   86:14+   F 15 '81.   K. Emerson
     *(Color blue)*      *(Color yellow)*  *(Color brown)*  *(Color purple)*     *(Color orange)*

FIG. 46.   Index entry for book reviews

Copyright © 1981 by The H. W. Wilson Company. Reprinted from *Abridged Readers' Guide to Periodical Literature* 47(3):251 (May 1981) by permission of the publisher.

colored orange in your sample. This book review was written by (K. Emerson).

By now you should understand what the *Abridged Readers' Guide to Periodical Literature* is and how it can help you find articles in magazines. Now, I'll let you try to find some articles. Using the copy of the *Abridged Readers' Guide to Periodical Literature* that is in front of you, find an article on the subject (*choose a subject heading from the issue you are using*).

(*Tone*) You should have found the article, (*give the title*), under the subject (*give subject heading*) on page (*specify*) of your copy of the *Abridged Readers' Guide*. If you found it easily, you are ready for the worksheet. If you had trouble, play through the tape again or review the illustrations in your booklet. When you feel you are ready, get a copy of the worksheet from (*your name*). Good luck!

[End of Script]

## WORKSHEET

Use your copy of the Abridged Readers' Guide to Periodical Literature to help you answer the questions about the entry below that was taken from the Abridged Readers' Guide.

```
SPORTS

    See also
    College athletics
    Recreation
            Competitions

    Flying high! [gymnasts at the Junior Olympics]
      C. Rindner.  il  Seventeen 40:46 Ap '81
```

1. Magazine Name _____

2. Subject _____

3. Date _____

4. See also Subjects _____

   _____

5. Article Title _____

6. Volume _____

7. Author _____

8. Subheading _____

9. Page Number _____

10. What is "Flying High" about? _____

    _____

# 7 ALMANACS

All students need to become familiar with the almanac as a source of ready reference. It is one of the few reference tools priced within the means of most families and most often available for reference in the home setting. The facts and statistics available in the almanac are those most often needed by a student.

In this kit, the student will gain insight into the types of materials found in an almanac and will learn to locate the desired information by using the index. The student will analyze subject entries and will recognize the function of asterisks and footnotes.

## Materials Needed:

1 Almanac (Sample used: *The World Almanac & Book of Facts*, 1981)
3 Colored pencils (red, blue, and green)
1 Felt-tip pen (black)
1 Two- or three-ring notebook binder
1 Blank cassette tape
1 Mimeo or ditto master.

## Preparing the Visual Book:

1. Use a copy machine to transfer the following almanac pages:
   a. Index page (*see* fig. 47)
   b. Page demonstrating subject heading shown on index page (*see* fig. 54)
   c. Page or pages demonstrating subheadings of subject used in fig. 54 (*see* figs. 55, 56, and 57)
   d. Page demonstrating use of asterisk (*see* fig. 58)
   e. Page demonstrating footnote numbers (*see* fig. 59)
   f. First page of multiple page subject (*see* fig. 61)
   g. Page where needed material is found in multiple page listing (*see* fig. 61).
2. Trim pages and mount on 8½″ x 11″ paper sheets.
3. If desired, copy mounted pages to eliminate loose edges.
4. Label and mark as shown in illustrations.
5. Type the following:
   a. Complete subject entry. Label (*see* fig. 48)
   b. Subject heading where only subheadings have page numbers indexed (*see* fig. 49)
   c. Subject heading with a descriptor (*see* fig. 50)

d. Optional: Subject heading with date qualifier (*see* fig. 51)

e. Optional: Subject heading for an organization with acronym or initialism (*see* fig. 52)

f. Two kinds of "see" references or a "see" and "see also" reference (*see* fig. 53)

g. Index entry for a subject with multiple pages (*see* fig. 60).

6. Laminate the pages or insert into plastic protective sheaths for durability.

7. Punch two or three holes in each page.

8. Put figures 47–61 into notebook binder in proper sequence indicated by numerical order.

# Preparing the Script:

1. Read the script and select and/or substitute the terminology congruent with that used in your library/media center.

2. Choose Option 1A or 1B and Option 4A or 4B to conform to your almanac.

3. Decide if Options (2 and 5), (3 and 6), 7, and 8 are used in your almanac. Mark script accordingly.

4. If using samples other than those illustrated, make changes where necessary in the script.

5. Proofread the script to correct any oversights or errors.

6. Record the script onto the blank cassette tape.

# Preparing the Worksheet:

1. Type the worksheet as it is written if you are using *The World Almanac & Book of Facts*, 1981

or

2. Substitute similar questions from the almanac you are using.

# Preparing for Student Use:

1. Arrange a table and chair.

2. Put the recorded tape cassette into a cassette player with earphones.

3. Put a copy of the almanac used in the illustrations on the table.

4. Give the student the visual book.

# Script

Today, you are going to learn to use an almanac. An almanac is a reference book that will help you find facts quickly. Many times you need to find specific information about a person, place, or thing and the best place to begin your search is in the almanac.

At (*name of school*), our almanacs are located (*describe the location*). The almanacs that we have in our (library/media center) are the (*name your almanacs*). A copy of (*The World Almanac & Book of Facts*) is on the table in front of you. This is the almanac you will be using today.

Look at the cover of the almanac. Notice that the year (1981) is printed on the cover. Almanacs must be rewritten every year because so much of the information we use them for changes each year. An almanac contains lists of facts and short articles about many different subjects. Among the interesting topics you can find in the almanac are: awards and prizes, actors and actresses, and television. Turn the almanac over and look at the back cover of (*The World Almanac*). (*Tone*) The subjects you see listed are just a few of those that you can find in an almanac. There are many, many others, as you will discover.

The place to begin your search for almanac information is in the index. Some almanacs put the index in the back of the book, while others have the index in front. (*The World Almanac & Book of Facts*) is an almanac with the index in

GUIDE
LETTERS
*(Color red)*

SUBJECT
HEADINGS
*(Color blue)*

SUBHEADINGS
*(Color green)*

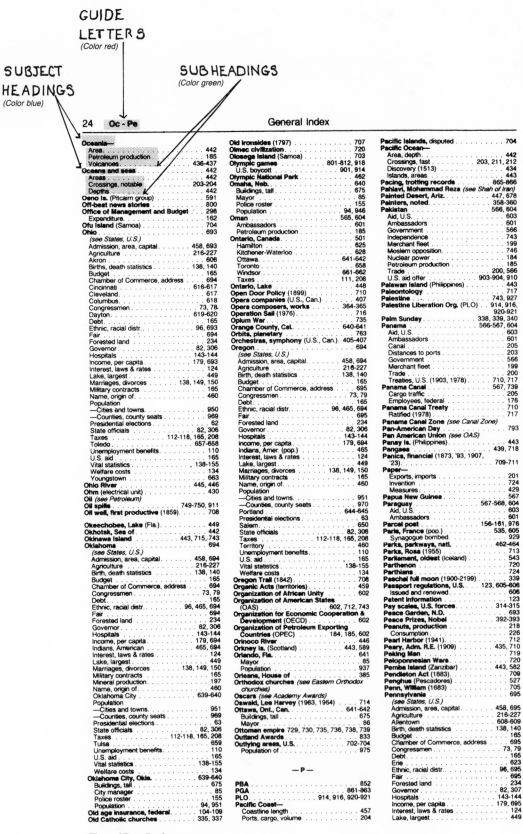

FIG. 47.    Index page

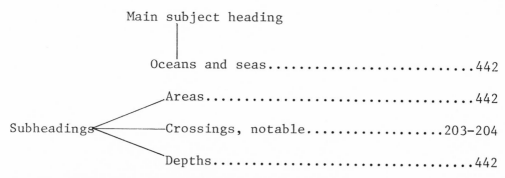

FIG. 48.   Index entry—main subject heading with subheads

(front). Open the copy of (*The World Almanac*) that is in front of you and find the page on which the index begins. (*Tone*) The index in (*The World Almanac & Book of Facts*) begins on page (3). To use the index properly, you must know how the index works. To help you learn to use the almanac index, we will talk about some samples in your booklet. Turn to page 1 (*see* fig. 47) in your booklet. (*Pause*)

*OPTION 1A: Index guide letters*

At the top of this sample index page, and colored red to help you, are a set of guide letters. The guide letters, located on the left hand side of the page, are (capital O and small c and capital P and small e). All of the subjects indexed on this page will begin with letters falling alphabetically between O c and P e). The subject (oil), is found on this page because (o i) comes between (o c and p e).

A single letter, (P), located (in the middle column toward the bottom of the page), shows you where the (Os) end and the (Ps) begin.

*OPTION 1B: No index guide letters*

All subject headings in the index of this almanac are in alphabetical order. Each letter of the alphabet is printed in large type to show you where words beginning with one letter end and where those beginning with the next letter start. When you use the index, first look for the letter of the alphabet that your subject word begins with and then look for the subject alphabetically. (Oceans) will be found alphabetically in the (O) section after the letter (O).

[End of Option 1]

Main subject headings are in alphabetical order in the almanac index. They are printed in dark or bold type so that they stand out on the page. The first two main subject entries on your sample page are colored blue to help you find the main headings.

Many of the subjects in the index have subheadings listed under the main heading. The subheadings for (the first) two subjects are colored green. The subheadings are also in alphabetical order under the main subject heading. Let's look more closely at some of the subjects on these index pages. Turn to page 2 (fig. 48) in your booklet. (*Pause*) In the sample on page 2 of your booklet, the main subject entry is (Oceans and Seas). The index tells you that information on the subject (Oceans and Seas) will be found on page (442) of the almanac.

Under the subject heading (Oceans and Seas), there are (three) subheadings. The subheadings will help you find special facts about (Oceans and Seas). The exact page where you will find the subheading information is given. For instance, under the subject heading (Oceans and Seas), the first subheading listed is (Areas). (How many miles of earth are covered by oceans and seas) will be found on page (442). The second subheading listed under (Oceans and Seas) is (Crossings, notable). Pages (203 and 204) will answer your questions about (ships that crossed the oceans on famous voyages). If you want to know (how deep the oceans and seas are), the subheading (Depths) tells you that this information will be found on page (442).

Let's go on to page 3 (fig. 49) in your booklet. (*Pause*) This is an index entry for (Pole vaulting records). Notice that no page number is given beside the main subject heading. Instead, you

```
Pole vaulting records--

    Olympic............................803

    World..............................858
```

FIG. 49.   Index entry for information to be found
under differing subject headings

must look at the subheadings. (Pole vaulting records) are listed for the subheadings only.

The (dash) following the subject heading tells you that there won't be an almanac entry for this main subject heading. Instead, you must look at the subheading to find the page you want. There are (two) subheadings for the subject (Pole vaulting records [dash]). The first subheading is (Olympic). This subheading tells you that (the record for the Olympic pole vault) will be found on page (803). The (second) subheading, (World), tells you that (the world record for pole vaulting) will be found on page (858).

Turn to page 4 (fig. 50) of your booklet. (*Pause*) Here is an index entry for (Pluto). After the subject heading (Pluto), you see the word (planet in parenthesis). This tells you that the almanac information on (Pluto) is about the (planet), not the (cartoon character).

*OPTION 2: Dates in index subject entries*
Go on to page 5 (fig. 51). Some index entries

look like this one for the (Oregon Trail). There is a date following the subject heading (Oregon Trail). (1842) was the year in which the (Oregon Trail began to be used). The index tells you that information on the (Oregon Trail) is on page (708). You will need to remember the date (1842) when you turn to page (708). The date will be necessary to help you find the information on the (Oregon Trail).
[End of Option 2]

*OPTION 3: Acronyms following organization names in index*
You are ready for page 6 (fig. 52). (*Pause*) Here is an index entry for the (Organization of Petroleum Exporting Countries). The (Organization of Petroleum Exporting Countries) is often called by its initials (O-PEC). The capital letters (O-P-E-C), written after the name, let you know what this organization is usually called.
[End of Option 3]

```
Pluto (planet).......................763
```

FIG. 50.   Index entry with word in parenthesis

```
Oregon Trail (1842)......................708
```

FIG. 51.   Index entry with date in parenthesis

```
Organization of Petroleum Exporting

    Countries (OPEC)..........184, 185, 602
```

FIG. 52.   Acronym in parenthesis following
organization name in index entry

*OPTION 4A: Almanac using "see" references only*

Let's go on to page (7) (fig. 53). When you learned to use the card catalog and the (*Children's Magazine Guide* and/or the *Abridged Readers' Guide to Periodical Literature*), you learned that there were "see" and "see also" references. (*The World Almanac*) uses the word "see" for both types of references.

Look at the subject heading (Ohio). Right under the subject heading (Ohio) are the words (see States, U.S.). After the (see States, U.S.), there is a long list of subheadings. You will find information on (Ohio) by looking for the pages listed for the subheadings. Even more information can be found, however, if you also look for the subject, (States, U.S.).

At the bottom of page (7), you see the subject (Oscars). The subject heading (Oscars) is followed by the words in parenthesis (see Academy Awards). No page number is given for the subject (Oscars). The only way you will find information about (Oscars) is by looking for the subject heading (Academy Awards) in the index.

*OPTION 4B: Almanac using "see" and "see also" references*

When you learned to use the card catalog and the (*Children's Magazine Guide* and/or the *Abridged Readers' Guide to Periodical Literature*), you learned about "see" and "see also" references.

Look at page (7) in your booklet. At the top of the page is a "see" reference. The subject heading is (*give a "see from" subject heading*). The subject heading (*specify*) is followed by the words see (*name the "see" subject or subjects*). The only way you will find information about (*give the "see from" subject*) is by looking for the subject heading (*give the "see" subject*).

At the bottom of page (7) in your booklet, is a "see also" reference. The subject (*give a subject with a "see also" reference*), has a page listed where you will find information about (*specify*). The "see also" reference tells you that you will find additional information on (*name the subject*) by looking for the "see also" reference (*give the "see also" listing*).

[End of Option 4]

```
Ohio.........................................693

    (see States, U.S.)

    Admission, area, capital.............458,693

    Agriculture..........................216-227

    Akron....................................608

    Births, death statistics.............138,140

    Budget...................................165

    Chamber of Commerce, address.............694

    Cincinnati...........................616-617

    Cleveland................................617

    Columbus.................................618

----------------------------------------------------------------

    Oscars (See Academy Awards)
```

Fig. 53.  Index "see" references

Now, let's see if you can put what you have learned about using the almanac index to work. Turn to index pages (12 and 13) in your copy of (*The World Almanac*).

*OPTION 5: To be used with Option 1A—guide letters*
What are the guide letters for page (12)? (*Pause*) If you said that the guide letters are (D i to E m), you are right!
[End of Option 5]

On what pages will you find information about (Amelia Earhart, the famous pilot)? That's spelled (E-a-r-h-a-r-t). (*Pause*) Did you find that page(s) (211 and 217) of the almanac will tell you about (Amelia Earhart)? What are the subheadings given for the subject (Earthquakes)? (*Pause*) There are (two) subheadings for (Earthquakes). The subheadings are (Causes) and (San Francisco).

*OPTION 6: To be used with Option 2—dates*
What year was the (first Earth Day celebrated)? (*Pause*) If you found that the (first Earth Day was celebrated in 1970), you are really doing very well!
[End of Option 6]

One last question. On what page will you find information on (ecology)? (*Pause*) No pages are given for the subject (Ecology), but the index tells you to see the subject (Environment). When you look for the subject (Environment) in the index, you find that the information will be found on page(s) (232 to 239) of the almanac.

By now you should understand how to use the index. Let's go on and take a look at some of the information in the almanac. The first index entry you looked at was (Oceans and Seas). The index told you that information about (Oceans and Seas) would be on page (442). Let's look at a copy of page (442). It is on page (8) (fig. 54) of your booklet.

I have typed the index entry below the sample page so you can compare the index entry and the page itself. The main subject heading in the index is (Oceans and Seas). Look at the top of this sample page. Each page of the almanac has a heading to help you. The heading for this page is (World Facts—Oceans; Continents). The heading, colored blue on your page, tells you

that this page will indeed give you facts about (Oceans). A line shows you that the page given in the index is the correct page in the almanac.

Turn to page (9) (fig. 55) in your booklet. (*Pause*) The first subheading in the index is (Areas). It has been colored green in the index entry. The section on page (442) where this information will be found also has been colored green. Notice that a line has been drawn from the page number in the index subheading to the number of the almanac page to show you that this is the correct page.

Let's look at the information in this section. By looking at the (number of square miles), you see that (the Pacific Ocean is the largest body of water in the world). (How many of the bodies of water listed on this page are actually oceans?) (*Pause*) Did you discover that (the only ones called oceans are the Pacific, Atlantic, Indian, and Arctic)?

(How many square miles does the Atlantic Ocean cover?) (*Pause*) If you found that the (Atlantic Ocean covers 33 million 420 thousand square miles), you are doing great!

Go on to page (10) (fig. 56). (*Pause*) The second subheading in the index entry for (Oceans and Seas) is (Crossings, notable). This subheading is again colored green. Notice that the page numbers given for this subheading about (notable ocean crossings) are (203 and 204). The section of the almanac page where you will find this information has been colored green.

Turn to page (11) (fig. 57). The third subheading under (Oceans and Seas) in the index is (Depths). This subheading is colored green too. A line shows you that page (442) is the page on which you will find information about (how deep the oceans are). The sections that tell about the (depth of the oceans) have been colored green. The sections, ("How Deep Is the Ocean" and "Ocean Areas and Average Depths") both give information about the subject (Ocean Depths). Look at the section labeled (Ocean Areas and Average Depths). (Which ocean or sea is the shallowest?) (*Pause*) If you said (the Yellow Sea is the most shallow body of water listed), you are using the facts on this page correctly.

Now turn to page (12) (fig. 58). When you were learning to use the index, you looked at the subject (Pole vaulting records [dash]). The index told you that you would find the (world record for the pole vault) on page (858). Look at the heading at the top of the page. The heading

442

## How Deep Is the Ocean?

Principal ocean depths. **Source:** Defense Mapping Agency Hydrographic/Topographic Center

| Name of area | Location | Meters | Depth Fathoms | Feet | Ship and/or country | Year |
|---|---|---|---|---|---|---|
| **Pacific Ocean** | | | | | | |
| Mariana Trench | 11°21'N, 142°12'E | 11,034 | 6,033 | 36,198 | Vityaz (USSR). | 1957 |
| Tonga Trench | 23°15.3'S, 174°44.7'W | 10,882 | 5,950 | 35,702 | Vityaz (USSR). | 1957 |
| Kuril Trench | 44°15.2'N, 150°34.2'E | 10,542 | 5,764 | 34,587 | Vityaz (USSR). | 1954 |
| Philippine Trench | 10°24'N, 126°40'E | 10,539 | 5,763 | 34,578 | Galathea (Danish) | 1951 |
| Izu Trench | 30°32'N, 142°31'E | 10,374 | 5,673 | 34,033 | USS Ramapo. | 1932 |
| Kermadec Trench | 31°52.8'S, 177°20.6'W | 10,047 | 5,494 | 32,964 | Vityaz (USSR). | 1957 |
| Bonin Trench. | 24°30'N, 143°24'E | 9,156 | 5,005 | 30,032 | Vityaz (USSR). | 1964 |
| New Britain Trench | 06°34'S, 153°55'E | 9,140 | 4,998 | 29,988 | Planet (German) | 1910 |
| Yap Trench. | 08°33'N, 138°02'E | 8,527 | 4,662 | 27,976 | Vityaz (USSR). | 1958 |
| Japan Trench | 36°08'N, 142°43'E | 8,412 | 4,597 | 27,591 | Bathymetric Map (USSR) | 1964 |
| Palau Trench. | 07°40'N, 135°04'E | 8,138 | 4,449 | 26,693 | Stefan (Germany). | 1905 |
| Aleutian Trench | 50°53'N, 176°23'E | 8,100 | 4,429 | 26,574 | USCGC Bering Strait. | 1953 |
| Peru Chile Trench | 23°18'S, 71°41'W | 8,064 | 4,409 | 26,454 | R/V Spencer F. Baird | 1957 |
| (Atacama Trench) | 23°27'S, 71°21'W | 8,064 | 4,409 | 26,454 | IGY. | |
| New Hebrides Trench. | 20°36'S, 168°37'E | 7,570 | 4,138 | 24,830 | Planet (German) | 1910 |
| Ryukyu Trench | 25°15'N, 128°32'E | 7,507 | 4,105 | 24,629 | Mansyu (Japan). | 1925 |
| Mid. America Trench | 14°02'N, 93°39'W | 6,669 | 3,642 | 21,852 | USS Epce | 1965 |
| **Atlantic Ocean** | | | | | | |
| Puerto Rico Trench | 19°55'N, 68°17'W | 8,648 | 4,729 | 28,374 | SS Archerfish | 1961 |
| Cayman Trench | 19°12'N, 80°00'W | 7,535 | 4,120 | 24,720 | R/V Vema (U.S.) | 1960 |
| So. Sandwich Trench | 55°14'S, 26°29'W | 8,252 | 4,512 | 27,072 | USS Eltanin | 1963 |
| Romanche Gap | 00°16'S, 18°35'W | 7,864 | 4,300 | 25,800 | R/V Vema | 1957 |
| Brazil Basin | 09°10'S, 23°02'W | 6,119 | 3,346 | 20,076 | R/V Vema (U.S.) | 1956 |
| **Indian Ocean** | | | | | | |
| Java Trench | 10°15'S, 109°E (approx.) | 7,725 | 4,224 | 25,344 | Natl Geographic. | 1967 |
| Ob Trench | (no position) | 6,874 | 3,759 | 22,553 | Nat'l Geographic | 1967 |
| Vema Trench | (no position) | 6,402 | 3,501 | 21,004 | Nat'l Geographic | 1967 |
| Agulhas Basin | (no position) | 6,195 | 3,388 | 20,325 | Nat'l Geographic | 1967 |
| Diamantina Trench | 35°00'S, 105°25'E | 6,062 | 3,315 | 19,800 | Nat'l Geographic | 1967 |
| **Arctic Ocean** | | | | | | |
| Eurasia Basin | 82°23'N, 19°31'E | 5,450 | 2,980 | 17,880 | Fidor Lithke (USSR) | 1955 |
| **Mediterranean Sea** | | | | | | |
| Ionian Basin | 36°32'N, 21°06'E | 5,150 | 2,816 | 16,896 | USS Tanner, | 1955 |

## Ocean Areas and Average Depths

Four major bodies of water are recognized by geographers and mapmakers. They are: the Pacific, Atlantic, Indian, and Arctic oceans. The Atlantic and Pacific oceans are considered divided at the equator into the No. and So. Atlantic; the No. and So. Pacific. The Arctic Ocean is the name for waters north of the continental land masses in the region of the Arctic Circle.

| | Sq. miles | Avg. depth in feet | | Sq. miles | Avg. depth in feet |
|---|---|---|---|---|---|
| Pacific Ocean | 64,186,300 | 13,739 | Hudson Bay | 281,900 | 305 |
| Atlantic Ocean. | 33,420,000 | 12,257 | East China Sea | 256,600 | 620 |
| Indian Ocean. | 28,350,500 | 12,704 | Andaman Sea | 218,100 | 3,667 |
| Arctic Ocean. | 5,105,700 | 4,362 | Black Sea | 196,100 | 3,906 |
| South China Sea | 1,148,500 | 4,802 | Red Sea | 174,900 | 1,764 |
| Caribbean Sea | 971,400 | 8,448 | North Sea | 164,900 | 308 |
| Mediterranean Sea | 969,100 | 4,926 | Baltic Sea | 147,500 | 180 |
| Bering Sea | 873,000 | 4,893 | Yellow Sea. | 113,500 | 121 |
| Gulf of Mexico | 582,100 | 5,297 | Persian Gulf | 88,800 | 328 |
| Sea of Okhotsk | 537,500 | 3,192 | Gulf of California | 59,100 | 2,375 |
| Sea of Japan | 391,100 | 5,468 | | | |

The Malayan Sea is not considered a geographical entity but a term used for convenience for waters between the South Pacific and the Indian Ocean.

## Continental Statistics

**Source:** National Geographic Society, Washington, D.C.

| Continents | Area (sq. mi.) | % of Earth | Population (est.) | % World total | Highest point (in feet) | Lowest point |
|---|---|---|---|---|---|---|
| Asia | 16,998,000 | 29.7 | 2,628,500,000 | 59.5 | Everest, 29,028 | Dead Sea, −1,312 |
| Africa | 11,682,000 | 20.4 | 472,000,000 | 10.7 | Kilimanjaro, 19,340 | Lake Assal, −512 |
| North America | 9,366,000 | 16.3 | 368,000,000 | 8.3 | McKinley, 20,320 | Death Valley, −282 |
| South America | 6,881,000 | 12.0 | 239,000,000 | 5.4 | Aconcagua, 22,834 | Valdes Penin., −131 |
| Europe. | 4,017,000 | 7.0 | 684,500,000 | 15.5 | El'brus, 18,510 | Caspian Sea, −92 |
| Australia. | 2,966,000 | 5.2 | 14,600,000 | 0.3 | Kosciusko, 7,316 | Lake Eyre, −52 |
| Antarctica | 5,100,000 | 8.9 | — | — | Vinson Massif, 16,860 | Not Known |
| **Est. World Population** | | | 4,414,000,000 | | | |

Oceans and seas.................442

(Color blue)

Areas.........................442

Crossings, notable........203–204

Depths.......................442

FIG. 54.   Comparison of text page heading with index main entry

(442)                  World Facts — Oceans; Continents

## How Deep Is the Ocean?

Principal ocean depths. **Source:** Defense Mapping Agency Hydrographic/Topographic Center

| Name of area | Location | | Meters | Depth Fathoms | Feet | Ship and/or country | Year |
|---|---|---|---|---|---|---|---|
| **Pacific Ocean** | | | | | | | |
| Mariana Trench | 11°21'N, | 142°12'E | 11,034 | 6,033 | 36,198 | Vityaz (USSR) | 1957 |
| Tonga Trench | 23°15.3'S, | 174°44.7'W | 10,882 | 5,950 | 35,702 | Vityaz (USSR) | 1957 |
| Kuril Trench | 44°15.2'N, | 150°34.2'E | 10,542 | 5,764 | 34,587 | Vityaz (USSR) | 1954 |
| Philippine Trench | 10°24'N, | 126°40'E | 10,539 | 5,763 | 34,578 | Galathea (Danish) | 1951 |
| Izu Trench | 30°32'N, | 142°31'E | 10,374 | 5,673 | 34,033 | USS Ramapo | 1932 |
| Kermadec Trench | 31°52.8'S, | 177°20.6'W | 10,047 | 5,494 | 32,964 | Vityaz (USSR) | 1957 |
| Bonin Trench | 24°30'N, | 143°24'E | 9,156 | 5,005 | 30,032 | Vityaz (USSR) | 1964 |
| New Britain Trench | 06°34'S, | 153°55'E | 9,140 | 4,998 | 29,988 | Planet (German) | 1910 |
| Yap Trench | 08°33'N, | 138°02'E | 8,527 | 4,662 | 27,976 | Vityaz (USSR) | 1958 |
| Japan Trench | 36°08'N, | 142°43'E | 8,412 | 4,597 | 27,591 | Bathymetric Map (USSR) | 1964 |
| Palau Trench | 07°40'N, | 135°04'E | 8,138 | 4,449 | 26,693 | Stefan (Germany) | 1905 |
| Aleutian Trench | 50°53'N, | 176°23'E | 8,100 | 4,429 | 26,574 | USCGC Bering Strait | 1953 |
| Peru Chile Trench | 23°18'S, | 71°41'W | 8,064 | 4,409 | 26,454 | R/V Spencer F. Baird | 1957 |
| (Atacama Trench) | 23°27'S, | 71°21'W | 8,064 | 4,409 | 26,454 | IGY | |
| New Hebrides Trench | 20°36'S, | 168°37'E | 7,570 | 4,138 | 24,830 | Planet (Germany) | 1910 |
| Ryukyu Trench | 25°15'N, | 128°32'E | 7,507 | 4,105 | 24,629 | Mansyu (Japan) | 1925 |
| Mid. America Trench | 14°02'N, | 93°39'W | 6,669 | 3,642 | 21,852 | USS Epce | 1965 |
| **Atlantic Ocean** | | | | | | | |
| Puerto Rico Trench | 19°35'N, | 68°17'W | 8,648 | 4,729 | 28,374 | SS Archerfish | 1961 |
| Cayman Trench | 19°12'N, | 80°00'W | 7,535 | 4,120 | 24,720 | R/V Vema (U.S.) | 1960 |
| So. Sandwich Trench | 55°14'S, | 26°29'W | 8,252 | 4,512 | 27,072 | USS Eltanin | 1963 |
| Romanche Gap | 00°16'S, | 18°35'W | 7,864 | 4,300 | 25,800 | R/V Vema | 1957 |
| Brazil Basin | 09°10'S, | 23°02'W | 6,119 | 3,346 | 20,076 | R/V Vema (U.S.) | 1956 |
| **Indian Ocean** | | | | | | | |
| Java Trench | 10°15'S, | 109°E (approx.) | 7,725 | 4,224 | 25,344 | Natl Geographic | 1967 |
| Ob Trench | (no position) | | 6,874 | 3,759 | 22,553 | Nat'l Geographic | 1967 |
| Vema Trench | (no position) | | 6,402 | 3,501 | 21,004 | Nat'l Geographic | 1967 |
| Agulhas Basin | (no position) | | 6,195 | 3,388 | 20,325 | Nat'l Geographic | 1967 |
| Diamantina Trench | 35°00'S, | 105°35'E | 6,062 | 3,315 | 19,800 | Nat'l Geographic | 1967 |
| **Arctic Ocean** | | | | | | | |
| Eurasia Basin | 82°23'N, | 19°31'E | 5,450 | 2,980 | 17,880 | Fidor Lithke (USSR) | 1955 |
| **Mediterranean Sea** | | | | | | | |
| Ionian Basin | 36°32'N, | 21°06'E | 5,150 | 2,816 | 16,896 | USS Tanner | 1955 |

(Color green) ## Ocean Areas and Average Depths

Four major bodies of water are recognized by geographers and mapmakers. They are: the Pacific, Atlantic, Indian, and Arctic oceans. The Atlantic and Pacific oceans are considered divided at the equator into the No. and So. Atlantic; the No. and So. Pacific. The Arctic Ocean is the name for waters north of the continental land masses in the region of the Arctic Circle.

| | Sq. miles | Avg. depth in feet | | Sq. miles | Avg. depth in feet |
|---|---|---|---|---|---|
| Pacific Ocean | 64,186,300 | 13,739 | Hudson Bay | 281,900 | 305 |
| Atlantic Ocean | 33,420,000 | 12,257 | East China Sea | 256,600 | 620 |
| Indian Ocean | 28,350,500 | 12,704 | Andaman Sea | 218,100 | 3,667 |
| Arctic Ocean | 5,105,700 | 4,362 | Black Sea | 196,100 | 3,906 |
| South China Sea | 1,148,500 | 4,802 | Red Sea | 174,900 | 1,764 |
| Caribbean Sea | 971,400 | 8,448 | North Sea | 164,900 | 308 |
| Mediterranean Sea | 969,100 | 4,926 | Baltic Sea | 147,500 | 180 |
| Bering Sea | 873,000 | 4,893 | Yellow Sea | 113,500 | 121 |
| Gulf of Mexico | 582,100 | 5,297 | Persian Gulf | 88,800 | 328 |
| Sea of Okhotsk | 537,500 | 3,192 | Gulf of California | 59,100 | 2,375 |
| Sea of Japan | 391,100 | 5,468 | | | |

The Malayan Sea is not considered a geographical entity but a term used for convenience for waters between the South Pacific and the Indian Ocean.

## Continental Statistics

**Source:** National Geographic Society, Washington, D.C.

| Continents | Area (sq. mi.) | % of Earth | Population (est.) | % World total | Highest point (in feet) | Lowest point |
|---|---|---|---|---|---|---|
| Asia | 16,998,000 | 29.7 | 2,628,500,000 | 59.5 | Everest, 29,028 | Dead Sea, −1,312 |
| Africa | 11,682,000 | 20.4 | 472,000,000 | 10.7 | Kilimanjaro, 19,340 | Lake Assal, −512 |
| North America | 9,366,000 | 16.3 | 368,000,000 | 8.3 | McKinley, 20,320 | Death Valley, −282 |
| South America | 6,881,000 | 12.0 | 239,000,000 | 5.4 | Aconcagua,22,834 | Valdes Penin., −131 |
| Europe | 4,017,000 | 7.0 | 684,500,000 | 15.5 | El'brus, 18,510 | Caspian Sea, −92 |
| Australia | 2,966,000 | 5.2 | 14,600,000 | 0.3 | Kosciusko, 7,310 | Lake Eyre, −52 |
| Antarctica | 5,100,000 | 8.9 | — | — | Vinson Massif, 16,860 | Not Known |
| | **Est. World Population** | | 4,414,000,000 | | | |

Oceans and seas.....................442

Areas............................442
(Color green)

Crossings, notable..........203-204

Depths..........................442

FIG. 55.   Correlating text with first subentry

Trade and Transportation — Distances Between Ports; Ocean Passages    (203)

## Shortest Navigable Distances Between Ports

Source: Distances Between Ports. Defense Mapping Agency Hydrographic/Topographic Center

Distances shown are in nautical miles (1,852 meters or about 6,076.115 feet) To get statute miles, multiply by 1.15.

| TO | FROM New York | Montreal | Colon¹ |
|---|---|---|---|
| Algiers, Algeria | 3,617 | 3,600 | 4,745 |
| Amsterdam, Netherlands | 3,438 | 3,162 | 4,825 |
| Baltimore, Md. | 417 | 1,769 | 1,901 |
| Barcelona, Spain | 3,714 | 3,697 | 4,842 |
| Boston, Mass. | 386 | 1,308 | 2,157 |
| Buenos Aires, Argentina | 5,817 | 6,455 | 5,472 |
| Cape Town, S. Africa² | 6,786 | 7,118 | 6,494 |
| Cherbourg, France | 3,154 | 2,878 | 4,541 |
| Cobh, Ireland | 2,901 | 2,603 | 4,308 |
| Copenhagen, Denmark | 3,846 | 3,570 | 5,233 |
| Dakar, Senegal | 3,335 | 3,566 | 3,694 |
| Galveston, Tex. | 1,882 | 3,165 | 1,492 |
| Gibraltar³ | 3,204 | 3,187 | 4,332 |
| Glasgow, Scotland | 3,086 | 2,691 | 4,508 |
| Halifax, N.S. | 600 | 895 | 2,295 |
| Hamburg, W. Germany | 3,674 | 3,398 | 5,061 |
| Hamilton, Bermuda | 697 | 1,572 | 1,659 |
| Havana, Cuba | 1,186 | 2,473 | 998 |
| Helsinki, Finland | 4,309 | 4,033 | 5,696 |
| Istanbul, Turkey | 5,001 | 4,984 | 6,129 |
| Kingston, Jamaica | 1,474 | 2,690 | 551 |
| Lagos, Nigeria | 4,883 | 5,130 | 5,049 |
| Lisbon, Portugal | 2,972 | 2,943 | 4,152 |
| Marseille, France | 3,891 | 3,874 | 5,019 |
| Montreal, Quebec | 1,460 | | 3,126 |
| Naples, Italy | 4,181 | 4,164 | 5,309 |
| Nassau, Bahamas | 962 | 2,274 | 1,166 |
| New Orleans, La. | 1,708 | 2,991 | 1,389 |
| New York, N.Y. | | 1,460 | 1,974 |
| Norfolk, Va. | 294 | 1,700 | 1,779 |
| Oslo, Norway | 3,827 | 3,165 | 5,053 |
| Piraeus, Greece | 4,688 | 4,671 | 5,816 |
| Port Said, Egypt | 5,123 | 5,106 | 6,251 |
| Rio de Janeiro, Brazil | 4,770 | 5,354 | 4,367 |
| St. John's, Nfld. | 1,093 | 1,043 | 2,695 |
| San Juan, Puerto Rico | 1,399 | 2,445 | 993 |
| Southampton, England | 3,189 | 2,913 | 4,576 |

| TO | FROM San. Fran. | Vancouver | Panama¹ |
|---|---|---|---|
| Acapulco, Mexico | 1,833 | 2,613 | 1,426 |
| Anchorage, Alas. | 1,872 | 1,444 | 5,093 |
| Bombay, India | 9,794 | 9,578 | 12,962 |
| Calcutta, India | 8,991 | 8,728 | 12,154 |
| Colon, Panama¹ | 3,298 | 4,076 | 44 |
| Jakarta, Indonesia | 7,641 | 7,360 | 10,637 |
| Haiphong, Vietnam | 6,496 | 6,231 | 9,673 |
| Hong Kong | 6,044 | 5,777 | 9,195 |
| Honolulu, Hawaii | 2,091 | 2,423 | 4,685 |
| Los Angeles, Cal. | 371 | 1,161 | 2,913 |
| Manila, Philippines | 6,221 | 5,976 | 9,347 |
| Melbourne, Australia | 6,970 | 7,343 | 7,928 |
| Pusan, S. Korea | 4,914 | 4,623 | 8,074 |
| Ho Chi Min City, Vietnam | 6,878 | 6,664 | 10,017 |
| San Francisco, Cal. | | 814 | 3,245 |
| Seattle, Wash. | 807 | 125 | 4,020 |
| Shanghai, China | 5,396 | 5,110 | 8,566 |
| Singapore | 7,353 | 7,078 | 10,505 |
| Suva, Fiji | 4,749 | 5,143 | 6,325 |
| Valparaiso, Chile | 5,140 | 5,915 | 2,616 |
| Vancouver, B.C. | 812 | | 4,032 |
| Vladivostok, USSR | 4,563 | 4,378 | 7,741 |
| Yokohama, Japan | 4,536 | 4,262 | 7,682 |

| TO | FROM | Port Said | Cape Town² | Singapore |
|---|---|---|---|---|
| Bombay, India | | 3,049 | 4,616 | 2,441 |
| Calcutta, India | | 4,695 | 5,638 | 1,649 |
| Dar es Salaam, Tanzania | | 3,238 | 2,365 | 4,042 |
| Jakarta, Indonesia | | 5,293 | 5,276 | 525 |
| Hong Kong | | 6,462 | 7,006 | 1,454 |
| Kuwait | | 3,360 | 5,176 | 3,833 |
| Manila, Philippines | | 6,348 | 6,777 | 1,330 |
| Melbourne, Australia | | 7,842 | 5,963 | 3,844 |
| Ho Chi Min City, Vietnam | | 5,667 | 6,263 | 649 |
| Singapore | | 5,018 | 5,614 | |
| Yokohama, Japan | | 7,907 | 8,503 | 2,889 |

(1) Colon on the Atlantic is 44 nautical miles from Panama (port) on the Pacific. (2) Cape Town is 35 nautical miles northwest of the Cape of Good Hope. (3) Gibraltar (port) is 24 nautical miles east of the Strait of Gibraltar.

---

*(Color green)* ## Notable Ocean Passages by Ships

Compiled by N.R.P. Bonsor

### Sailing Vessels

| Date | Ship | From | To | Nautical miles | Time D. H. M | Speed (knots) |
|---|---|---|---|---|---|---|
| 1846 | Yorkshire | Liverpool | New York | 3150 | 16. 0. 0 | 8.46† |
| 1853 | Northern Light | San Francisco | Boston | — | 76. 6. 0 | — |
| 1854 | James Baines | Boston Light | Light Rock | — | 12. 6. 0 | — |
| 1854 | Flying Cloud | New York | San Francisco | 15091 | 89. 0. 0 | 7.07† |
| 1868-9 | Thermopylae | Liverpool | Melbourne | — | 63.18.15 | — |
| — | Red Jacket | New York | Liverpool | 3150 | 13. 1.25 | 10.05† |
| — | Starr King | 50 S. Lat | Golden Gate | — | 36. 0. 0 | — |
| — | Golden Fleece | Equator | San Francisco | — | 12.12. 0 | — |
| 1905 | Atlantic | Sandy Hook | England | 3013 | 12. 4. 0 | 10.32 |

### Atlantic Crossing by Passenger Steamships

| | | | | | | |
|---|---|---|---|---|---|---|
| 1819 (5/22 - 6/20) | Savannah (a) | US Savannah | Liverpool | — | 29. 4. 0 | — |
| 1838 (5/7 - 5/22) | Great Western | Br New York | Avonmouth | 3218 | 14.15.59 | 9.14 |
| 1840 (8/4 - 8/14) | Britannia | Br Halifax | Liverpool | 2610 | 9.21.44 | 10.98† |
| 1854 (6/28 - 7/7) | Baltic | US Liverpool | New York | 3037 | 9.16.52 | 13.04 |
| 1856 (8/6 - 8/15) | Persia | Br Sandy Hook | Liverpool | 3046 | 8.23.19 | 14.15† |
| 1876 (12/16-12/24) | Britannic | Br Sandy Hook | Queenstown | 2882 | 7.12.41 | 15.94 |
| 1895 (5/18 - 5/24) | Lucania | Br Sandy Hook | Queenstown | 2897 | 5.11.40 | 22.00 |
| 1898 (3/30 - 4/5) | Kaiser Wilhelm der Grosse | Ger Needles | Sandy Hook | 3120 | 5.20. 0 | 22.29 |
| 1901 (7/10 - 7/17) | Deutschland | Ger Sandy Hook | Eddystone | 3082 | 5.11. 5 | 23.51 |
| 1907 (10/6 - 10/10) | Lusitania | Br Queenstown | Sandy Hook | 2780 | 4.19.52 | 23.99 |
| 1924 (8/20 - 8/25) | Mauretania | Br Ambrose | Cherbourg | 3198 | 5. 1.49 | 26.25 |
| 1929 (7/17 - 7/22) | Bremen* | Ger Cherbourg | Ambrose | 3164 | 4.17.42 | 27.83 |
| 1933 (6/27 - 7/2) | Europa | Ger Cherbourg | Ambrose | 3149 | 4.16.48 | 27.92 |
| 1933 (8/11 - 8/16) | Rex | It Gibraltar | Ambrose | 3181 | 4.13.58 | 28.92 |
| 1935 (5/30 - 6/3) | Normandie* | Fr Bishop Rock | Ambrose | 2971 | 4. 3. 2 | 29.98 |
| 1938 (8/10 - 8/14) | Queen Mary | Br Ambrose | Bishop Rock | 2938 | 3.20.42 | 31.69 |
| 1952 (7/11 - 7/15) | United States | US Bishop Rock | Ambrose | 2906 | 3.12.12 | 34.51 |
| 1952 (7/3 - 7/7) | United States* (e) | US Ambrose | Bishop Rock | 2942 | 3.10.40 | 35.59 |

### Other Ocean Passages

| | | | | | | |
|---|---|---|---|---|---|---|
| 1928 (June) | USS Lexington | San Pedro | Honolulu | 2226 | 3. 0.36 | 30.66 |
| 1944 (Jul-Sep) | St. Roch (c) (Can) | Halifax | Vancouver | 7295 | 86. 0. 0 | — |
| 1945 (7/16-7/19) | USS Indianapolis (d) | San Francisco | Oahu, Hawaii | 2091 | 3. 2.20 | 28.07 |
| 1945 (11/26) | USS Lake Champlain | Gibraltar | Newport News | 3360 | 4. 8.51 | 32.04 |
| 1950 (Jul-Aug) | USS Boxer | Japan | San Francisco | 5000 | 7.18.36 | 26.80† |

*(continued)*

Oceans and seas.................442

Areas.......................442

Crossings, notable.........203-204
*(Color green)*

Depths.....................442

FIG. 56.  Correlating text with second subentry

(442)    World Facts — Oceans; Continents

## How Deep Is the Ocean?

Principal ocean depths. **Source:** Defense Mapping Agency Hydrographic/Topographic Center

| Name of area | Location | | Meters | Depth Fathoms | Feet | Ship and/or country | Year |
|---|---|---|---|---|---|---|---|
| **Pacific Ocean** | | | | | | | |
| Mariana Trench . . . . . . . . | 11°21'N, | 142°12'E . . . . | 11,034 | 6,033 | 36,198 | Vityaz (USSR) . . . . . . . . | 1957 |
| Tonga Trench . . . . . . . . | 23°15.3'S, | 174°44.7'W . . . . | 10,882 | 5,950 | 35,702 | Vityaz (USSR) . . . . . . . . | 1957 |
| Kuril Trench . . . . . . . | 44°15.2'N, | 150°34.2'E . . . . | 10,542 | 5,764 | 34,587 | Vityaz (USSR) . . . . . . . . | 1954 |
| Philippine Trench . . . . | 10°24'N, | 126°40'E . . . . | 10,539 | 5,763 | 34,578 | Galathea (Danish) . . . . . . . | 1951 |
| Izu Trench . . . . | 30°32'N, | 142°31'E . . . . | 10,374 | 5,673 | 34,033 | USS Ramapo . . . . . . . . . . | 1932 |
| Kermadec Trench . . . . . | 31°52.8'S, | 177°20.6'W . . . . | 10,047 | 5,494 | 32,964 | Vityaz (USSR) . . . . . . . . | 1957 |
| Bonin Trench . . . . . . | 24°30'N, | 143°24'E . . . . | 9,156 | 5,005 | 30,032 | Vityaz (USSR) . . . . . . . . | 1964 |
| New Britain Trench . . . . | 06°34'S, | 153°55'E . . . . | 9,140 | 4,998 | 29,988 | Planet (German) . . . . . . . | 1910 |
| Yap Trench . . . . . . | 08°33'N, | 138°02'E . . . . | 8,527 | 4,662 | 27,976 | Vityaz (USSR) . . . . . . . . | 1958 |
| Japan Trench . . . . | 36°08'N, | 142°43'E . . . . | 8,412 | 4,597 | 27,591 | Bathymetric Map (USSR) . . . | 1964 |
| Palau Trench . . . . . | 07°40'N, | 135°04'E . . . . | 8,138 | 4,449 | 26,693 | Stefan (Germany) . . . . . . . | 1905 |
| Aleutian Trench . . . . | 50°53'N, | 176°23'E . . . . | 8,100 | 4,429 | 26,574 | USCGC Bering Strait . . . . . | 1953 |
| Peru Chile Trench . . . . | 23°18'S, | 71°41'W . . . . | 8,064 | 4,409 | 26,454 | R/V Spencer F. Baird . . . . . | 1957 |
| (Atacama Trench) . . . | 23°27'S, | 71°21'W . . . . | 8,064 | 4,409 | 26,454 | IGY . . . . . . . . . . . | |
| New Hebrides Trench . . . | 20°36'S, | 168°37'E . . . . | 7,570 | 4,138 | 24,830 | Planet (Germany) . . . . . . . | 1910 |
| Ryukyu Trench . . . . . . | 25°15'N, | 128°32'E . . . . | 7,507 | 4,105 | 24,629 | Mansyu (Japan) . . . . . . . | 1925 |
| Mid. America Trench . . . . | 14°02'N, | 93°39'W . . . . | 6,669 | 3,642 | 21,852 | USS Epce . . . . . . . . . | 1965 |
| **Atlantic Ocean** | | | | | | | |
| Puerto Rico Trench . . . . | 19°35'N, | 68°17'W . . . . | 8,648 | 4,729 | 28,374 | SS Archerfish . . . . . . . . . | 1961 |
| Cayman Trench . . . . . . | 19°12'N, | 80°00'W . . . . | 7,535 | 4,120 | 24,720 | R/V Vema (U.S.) . . . . . . . | 1960 |
| So. Sandwich Trench . . . . | 55°14'S, | 26°29'W . . . . | 8,252 | 4,512 | 27,072 | USS Eltanin . . . . . . . . | 1963 |
| Romanche Gap . . . . . . . | 00°16'S, | 18°35'W . . . . | 7,864 | 4,300 | 25,800 | R/V Vema . . . . . . . . . | 1957 |
| Brazil Basin . . . . . . . . . | 09°16'S, | 23°02'W . . . . | 6,119 | 3,346 | 20,076 | R/V Vema (U.S.) . . . . . . . | 1956 |
| **Indian Ocean** | | | | | | | |
| Java Trench . . . . . . . . . | 10°15'S, | 109°E'(approx.) | 7,725 | 4,224 | 25,344 | Natl Geographic . . . . . . . . | 1967 |
| Ob Trench . . . . . . . . . . | (no position) | . . . . . . . . | 6,874 | 3,759 | 22,553 | Nat'l Geographic . . . . . . . . | 1967 |
| Vema Trench . . . . . . . . | (no position) | . . . . . . . . | 6,402 | 3,501 | 21,004 | Nat'l Geographic . . . . . . . . | 1967 |
| Agulhas Basin . . . . . . . | (no position) | . . . . . . . . | 6,195 | 3,388 | 20,325 | Nat'l Geographic . . . . . . . . | 1967 |
| Diamantina Trench . . . . . | 35°00'S, | 105°35'E . . . . | 6,062 | 3,315 | 19,800 | Nat'l Geographic . . . . . . . . | 1967 |
| **Arctic Ocean** | | | | | | | |
| Eurasia Basin . . . . . . . . | 82°23'N, | 19°31'E . . . . | 5,450 | 2,980 | 17,880 | Fidor Lithke (USSR) . . . . . . | 1955 |
| **Mediterranean Sea** | | | | | | | |
| Ionian Basin . . . . . . . . . | 36°32'N, | 21°06'E . . . . | 5,150 | 2,816 | 16,896 | USS Tanner, . . . . . . . . . | 1955 |

## Ocean Areas and Average Depths (Color green)

Four major bodies of water are recognized by geographers and mapmakers. They are: the Pacific, Atlantic, Indian, and Arctic oceans. The Atlantic and Pacific oceans are considered divided at the equator into the No. and So. Atlantic; the No. and So. Pacific. The Arctic Ocean is the name for waters north of the continental land masses in the region of the Arctic Circle.

| | Sq. miles | Avg. depth in feet | | Sq. miles | Avg. depth in feet |
|---|---|---|---|---|---|
| Pacific Ocean . . . . . . . . | 64,186,300 | 13,739 | Hudson Bay . . . . . . . . . | 281,900 | 305 |
| Atlantic Ocean . . . . . . . . | 33,420,000 | 12,257 | East China Sea . . . . . . . | 256,600 | 620 |
| Indian Ocean . . . . . . . | 28,350,500 | 12,704 | Andaman Sea . . . . . . . . | 218,100 | 3,667 |
| Arctic Ocean . . . . . . . . | 5,105,700 | 4,362 | Black Sea . . . . . . . . . | 196,100 | 3,906 |
| South China Sea . . . . . . | 1,148,500 | 4,802 | Red Sea . . . . . . . . . | 174,900 | 1,764 |
| Caribbean Sea . . . . . . | 971,400 | 8,448 | North Sea . . . . . . . . . | 164,900 | 308 |
| Mediterranean Sea . . . . . . | 969,100 | 4,926 | Baltic Sea . . . . . . . . . | 147,500 | 180 |
| Bering Sea . . . . . . . . | 873,000 | 4,893 | Yellow Sea . . . . . . . . . | 113,500 | 121 |
| Gulf of Mexico . . . . . . . | 582,100 | 5,297 | Persian Gulf . . . . . . . . | 88,800 | 328 |
| Sea of Okhotsk . . . . . . | 537,500 | 3,192 | Gulf of California . . . . . . | 59,100 | 2,375 |
| Sea of Japan . . . . . . . | 391,100 | 5,468 | | | |

The Malayan Sea is not considered a geographical entity but a term used for convenience for waters between the South Pacific and the Indian Ocean.

## Continental Statistics

**Source:** National Geographic Society, Washington, D.C.

| Continents | Area (sq. mi.) | % of Earth | Population (est.) | % World total | Highest point (in feet) | Lowest point |
|---|---|---|---|---|---|---|
| Asia . . . . . . . | 16,998,000 | 29.7 | 2,628,500,000 | 59.5 | Everest, 29,028 | Dead Sea, −1,312 |
| Africa . . . . . . | 11,682,000 | 20.4 | 472,000,000 | 10.7 | Kilimanjaro, 19,340 | Lake Assal, −512 |
| North America . . | 9,366,000 | 16.3 | 368,000,000 | 8.3 | McKinley, 20,320 | Death Valley, −282 |
| South America . . | 6,881,000 | 12.0 | 239,000,000 | 5.4 | Aconcagua, 22,834 | Valdes Penin., −131 |
| Europe . . . . . . | 4,017,000 | 7.0 | 684,500,000 | 15.5 | El'brus, 18,510 | Caspian Sea, −92 |
| Australia . . . . . . | 2,966,000 | 5.2 | 14,600,000 | 0.3 | Kosciusko, 7,310 | Lake Eyre, −52 |
| Antarctica . . . . | 5,100,000 | 8.9 | — | — | Vinson Massif, 16,860 | Not Known |
| **Est. World Population** | | | 4,414,000,000 | | | |

Oceans and seas . . . . . . . . . . . . . . . . . . 442

Areas . . . . . . . . . . . . . . . . . . . . . . . 442

Crossings, notable . . . . . . . . . . 203–204

(Color green) Depths . . . . . . . . . . . . . . . . . . . . . 442

FIG. 57.    Correlating text page information with third subentry

858        Sports — Track and Field Records; One-Mile Run; Table Tennis

**Field Events**

| Event | Record | Holder | Country | Date | Where made |
|---|---|---|---|---|---|
| High jump | *7 ft., 9 in. | Gerd Wessig | E. Germany | Aug. 1, 1980 | Moscow |
| Long jump | 29 ft., 2½ in. | Bob Beamon | U.S. | Oct. 18, 1968 | Mexico City |
| Triple jump | 58 ft., 8¼ in. | Joao de Oliveira | Brazil | Oct. 15, 1975 | Mexico City |
| Pole vault | *18 ft., 11½ in. | Wladyslaw Kozakiewicz | Poland | July 30, 1980 | Moscow |
| 16 lb. shot put | 72 ft., 8 in. | Udo Beyer | E. Germany | July 6, 1978 | Sweden |
| Discus throw | 233 ft., 5 in. | Wolfgang Schmidt | E. Germany | Aug. 9, 1978 | E. Berlin |
| Javelin throw | 310 ft., 4 in. | Miklos Nemeth | Hungary | July 26, 1976 | Montreal |
| 16 lb. hammer throw | *268 ft., 4½ in. | Yuri Sedykh | USSR | July 31, 1980 | Moscow |
| Decathlon | *8,649 pts. | Guido Kratschmer | W. Germany | June, 1980 | W. Germany |

## Women's Records

### Running

| | | | | | |
|---|---|---|---|---|---|
| 100 yards | 10.0 s. | Chi Cheng | Taiwan | June 13, 1970 | Portland, Ore. |
| 220 yards | 22.6 s. | Chi Cheng | Taiwan | July 3, 1970 | Los Angeles |
| 440 yards | 52.2 s. | Kathy Hammond | U.S. | Aug. 12, 1972 | Urbana, Ill. |
| | | Debra Sapenter | U.S. | June 29, 1974 | Bakersfield, Cal. |
| 880 yards | 2 m., 02.0 s. | Judy Pollock | Australia | July 5, 1967 | Sweden |
| | | Dixie Willis | Australia | Mar. 3, 1962 | Perth, Australia |
| 1 mile | *4 m., 21.7 s. | Mary Decker | U.S. | Jan. 26, 1980 | Auckland, N.Z. |
| 100 meters | *10.87 s. | Lyudmila Kondratyeva | USSR | June 3, 1980 | Moscow |
| 200 meters | 21.71 s. | Marita Koch | E. Germany | June 10, 1979 | E. Berlin |
| 400 meters | 48.60 s. | Marita Koch | E. Germany | Aug. 4, 1979 | Turin, Italy |
| 800 meters | *1 m., 53.5 s. | Nadezhda Olizarenko | USSR | July, 1980 | Moscow |
| 1,500 meters | *3 m., 55 s. | Tatyana Kazankina | USSR | July 6, 1980 | Moscow |
| 3,000 meters | 8 m., 27.1 s. | Ludmila Bragina | USSR | Aug. 7, 1976 | College Park, Md. |

### Hurdles

| | | | | | |
|---|---|---|---|---|---|
| 100 meters | *12.36 s. | Grazyna Rabsztyn | Poland | June, 1980 | Warsaw |
| 400 meters | *54.28 s. | Karin Rossley | E. Germany | May, 1980 | E. Germany |

### Field Events

| | | | | | |
|---|---|---|---|---|---|
| High jump | 6 ft., 7 in. | Sara Simeoni | Italy | Aug. 31, 1978 | Prague |
| Shot put | 73 ft., 2¾ in. | Helena Fibigerova | Czech. | Aug. 20, 1977 | Czech. |
| Long jump | 23 ft., 3¼ in. | Vilma Bardauskiene | USSR | Aug. 29, 1978 | Prague |
| Discus throw | *235 ft., 7 in. | Maria Vergova-Petkova | Bulgaria | July, 1980 | Sofia |
| Javelin | *229 ft., 11 in. | Tatyana Biryulina | USSR | July, 1980 | Podolsk, USSR |
| Pentathlon | *5,083 pts. | Nadyezhda Tkachenko | USSR | July, 1980 | Moscow |

### Relay Races

| | | | | | |
|---|---|---|---|---|---|
| 400 mtrs. (4×100) | *41.60 s. | National team | E. Germany | July, 1980 | Moscow |
| 800 mtrs. (4×200) | 1 m., 20.3 s. | National team | U.S. | May, 1978 | Tempe, Ariz. |
| 1,600 mtrs. (4×400) | 3 m., 19.2 s. | National team | E. Germany | July 31, 1976 | Montreal |
| 1 mile (4×440) | 3 m., 30.3 s. | National team (Krause, Jost, Weinstein, Barth) | W. Germany | July 19, 1975 | Durham, N.C. |

## Evolution of the World Record for the One-Mile Run

The table below shows how the world record for the one-mile has been lowered in the past 116 years.

| Year | Individual, country | Time | Year | Individual, country | Time |
|---|---|---|---|---|---|
| 1864 | Charles Lawes, Britain | 4:56 | 1937 | Sydney Wooderson, Britain | 4:06.4 |
| 1865 | Richard Webster, Britain | 4:36.5 | 1942 | Gunder Haegg, Sweden | 4:06.2 |
| 1868 | William Chinnery, Britain | 4:29 | 1942 | Arne Andersson, Sweden | 4:06.2 |
| 1868 | W. C. Gibbs, Britain | 4:28.8 | 1942 | Gunder Haegg, Sweden | 4:04.6 |
| 1874 | Walter Slade, Britain | 4:26 | 1943 | Arne Andersson, Sweden | 4:02.6 |
| 1875 | Walter Slade, Britain | 4:24.5 | 1944 | Arne Andersson, Sweden | 4:01.6 |
| 1880 | Walter George, Britain | 4:23.2 | 1945 | Gunder Haegg, Sweden | 4:01.4 |
| 1882 | Walter George, Britain | 4:21.4 | 1954 | Roger Bannister, Britain | 3:59.4 |
| 1882 | Walter George, Britain | 4:19.4 | 1954 | John Landy, Australia | 3:58 |
| 1884 | Walter George, Britain | 4:18.4 | 1957 | Derek Ibbotson, Britain | 3:57.2 |
| 1894 | Fred Bacon, Scotland | 4:18.2 | 1958 | Herb Elliott, Australia | 3:54.5 |
| 1895 | Fred Bacon, Scotland | 4:17 | 1962 | Peter Snell, New Zealand | 3:54.4 |
| 1895 | Thomas Conneff, U.S. | 4:15.6 | 1964 | Peter Snell, New Zealand | 3:54.1 |
| 1911 | John Paul Jones, U.S. | 4:15.4 | 1965 | Michel Jazy, France | 3:53.6 |
| 1913 | John Paul Jones, U.S. | 4:14.6 | 1966 | Jim Ryun, U.S. | 3:51.3 |
| 1915 | Norman Taber, U.S. | 4:12.6 | 1967 | Jim Ryun, U.S. | 3:51.1 |
| 1923 | Paavo Nurmi, Finland | 4:10.4 | 1975 | Filbert Bayi, Tanzania | 3:51 |
| 1931 | Jules Ladoumegue, France | 4:09.2 | 1975 | John Walker, New Zealand | 3:49.4 |
| 1933 | Jack Lovelock, New Zealand | 4:07.6 | 1979 | Sebastian Coe, Britain | 3:49 |
| 1934 | Glenn Cunningham, U.S. | 4:06.8 | 1980 | Steve Ovett, Britain | 3:48.8 |

## U.S. National Open Table Tennis Championships

Ft. Worth, Tex., June 26-29, 1980

**Men's Singles** — Mikael Appelgren, Sweden.
**Women's Singles** — Kayoko Kawahigashi, Japan.
**Mixed Doubles** — Si-Hung Yoo & Soo-Ja Lee, South Korea.
**Women's Doubles** — Kyung-Ja Kim & Soo-Ja Lee, South Ko-rea.
**Men's Doubles** — Dan & Rick Seemiller, Pittsburgh, Pa.
**Men's Team** — United States.
**Women's Team** — South Korea.

\* Indicates pending record; a number of new records
await confirmation.

Fig. 58.   Finding information on the almanac page

## 184    Energy — Nuclear Power; Electricity; Petroleum

### World Nuclear Power

Source: Energy Information Agency, U.S. Energy Department

| Country | Operational reactors | Capacity[1] | Generation[2] 1979 | Country | Operational reactors | Capacity[1] | Generation[2] 1979 |
|---|---|---|---|---|---|---|---|
| Argentina | 1 | 360 | 2.7 | Netherlands | 2 | 520 | 3.5 |
| Belgium | 3 | 1,740 | 11.4 | Pakistan | 1 | 140 | 0 |
| Canada | 8 | 5,590 | 38.4 | South Korea | 1 | 590 | 3.2 |
| Finland | 2 | 1,150 | 6.7 | Spain | 3 | 1,120 | 6.7 |
| France | 15 | 7,800 | 39.9 | Sweden | 6 | 3,850 | 21.0 |
| Germany, W. | 10 | 7,050 | 40.4 | Switzerland | 3 | 1,060 | 11.8 |
| Great Britain | 3 | 9,040 | 38.6 | Taiwan | 2 | 1,270 | 6.3 |
| India | 3 | 620 | 2.9 | U.S. | 71 | 54,180 | 270.7 |
| Italy | 4 | 1,490 | 2.6 | **Total[3]** | **189** | **110,410[4]** | **568.8** |
| Japan | 20 | 12,840 | 62.0 | | | | |

(1) Thousand kilowatts. (2) Billion kilowatt hours. (3) Non-Communist countries. (4) Total may not equal sum of components due to independent rounding.

### World Electricity Production

Source: UN Monthly Bulletin of Statistics, July 1980 (1979 production, in million kilowatt-hours.)

| Country | Production | Country | Production | Country | Production | Country | Production |
|---|---|---|---|---|---|---|---|
| U.S. | 2,247,652 | Italy | 180,522 | Sweden | 92,398 | Romania[4] | 59,856 |
| USSR | 1,239,998 | China[2] | 121,000 | Australia | 93,701 | Mexico[2] | 50,052 |
| Japan | 512,070 | Poland | 117,460 | South Africa[3] | 84,384 | Yugoslavia | 52,254 |
| W. Germany | 374,219 | Spain | 105,410 | Norway | 89,008 | Switzerland | 42,710 |
| Canada | 352,303 | E Germany | 106,060 | Czechoslovakia | 67,897 | Austria | 40,463 |
| United Kingdom | 299,960 | India | 95,952[2] | Netherlands | 64,457 | | |
| France | 241,124 | Brazil[1] | 99,864[4] | | | | |

(1) Estimated figures for Jan., March. (2) 1975 estimate. (3) 1978. (4) 1977.

### Production of Electricity in the U.S. by Source

Source: Energy Information Administration, U.S. Energy Department
Amounts include both privately-owned and publicly-owned utilities.

| Calendar Year | Net production (million kwh) | Coal | Oil | Gas | Nuclear | Hydro | Other[1] |
|---|---|---|---|---|---|---|---|
| 1971 | 1,612,593 | 44.3 | 13.6 | 23.2 | 2.4 | 16.5 | 0.05 |
| 1974 | 1,867,103 | 44.5 | 16.0 | 17.2 | 6.1 | 16.1 | 0.1 |
| 1975 | 1,917,638 | 44.5 | 15.1 | 15.6 | 9.0 | 15.6 | 0.2 |
| 1976 | 2,037,775 | 46.4 | 15.7 | 14.4 | 9.4 | 13.9 | 0.2 |
| 1977 | 2,124,580 | 46.4 | 16.8 | 14.4 | 11.8 | 10.4 | 0.2 |
| 1978 | 2,206,515 | 44.2 | 16.5 | 13.8 | 12.5 | 12.7 | 0.2 |
| 1979 | 2,247,372 | 47.8 | 13.5 | 14.7 | 11.4 | 12.4 | 0.2 |

(1) Includes electricity produced from geothermal power, wood, and waste.

### U.S. Petroleum Imports by Source

Source: Department of Energy
(in thousands of barrels per day)

| Nation | 1975 | 1976 | 1977 | 1978 | 1979 |
|---|---|---|---|---|---|
| Algeria | 288.2 | 438.3 | 565.2 | 632.1 | 630.5 |
| Indonesia | 437.7 | 569.4 | 576.2 | 538.2 | 416.9 |
| Iran | 524.8 | 546.5 | 786.4 | 544.7 | 303.2 |
| Libya | 329.3 | 529.3 | 837.7 | 641.1 | 654.0 |
| Nigeria | 837.8 | 1,119.2 | 1,229.6 | 904.7 | 1,077.6 |
| Saudi Arabia | 891.6 | 1,365.8 | 1,523.8 | 1,137.2 | 1,296.8 |
| United Arab Emirates | 154.2 | 323.2 | 446.3 | 635.5 | 691.1 |
| Venezuela | 1,090.1 | 218.0 | 378.1 | 224.0 | 212.2 |
| Other OPEC | 226.3 | | | | |
| **Total OPEC[2]** | **4,753.0** | **6,079.9** | **7,252.2** | **5,636.8** | **5,612.0** |
| Arab OPEC Members | 1,790.1 | 2,773.0 | 3,636.5 | 2,920.8 | 3,037.4 |
| Bahamas | 152.0 | 116.5 | 168.0 | 158.4 | 147.7 |
| Canada | 845.2 | 599.3 | 502.8 | 468.6 | 532.5 |
| Neth'lands Antilles | 323.6 | 274.6 | 218.3 | 317.8 | 291.3 |
| Puerto Rico | 89.7 | 88.1 | 102.8 | 89.4 | 186.3 |
| Trinidad/Tobago | 240.9 | 272.6 | 286.0 | 251.0 | 431.5 |
| Virgin Islands | 406.5 | 423.1 | 466.7 | 426.8 | 434.1 |
| Mexico | 30.4 | 87.1 | 179.3 | 649.9 | 744.0 |
| Other non-OPEC | 306.1 | 373.5 | 657.1 | | |
| **Total non-OPEC** | **2,435.4** | **2,234.0** | **2,583.0** | **2,591.5** | **2,799.1** |
| **Total Imports (avg.)** | **6,056.0** | **7,313.0** | **8,714.0** | **10,843.7** | **NA** |

(1) Ecuador, Gabon, Iraq, Kuwait, Qatar. (2) Imports do not add to totals because OPEC figures include petroleum transshipped through, and usually refined in, other countries and counted again as imports from those countries. NA-Not available.

## Energy — Crude Oil Production; Supply and Demand; U.S. Dependence    185

### World Production of Crude Oil
#### Twenty Leading Nations

(thousands of barrels)
Source: Energy Information Administration, U.S. Energy Dept.

| | 1978 | | | 1979 | |
|---|---|---|---|---|---|
| Nation | Production | % of total world production | Nation | Production | % of total world production |
| 1. USSR | 4,093,475 | 18.5% | 1. USSR | 4,186,550 | 18.6% |
| 2. United States | 3,175,927 | 14.3 | 2. Saudi Arabia | 3,374,425 | 14.7 |
| 3. Saudi Arabia | 3,113,470 | 14.0 | 3. United States | 3,111,625 | 13.7 |
| 4. Iran | 1,900,555 | 8.6 | 4. Iran | 1,253,775 | 5.5 |
| 5. Iraq | 959,585 | 4.3 | 5. Iraq | 1,107,775 | 5.0 |
| 6. Venezuela | 790,418 | 3.6 | 6. Venezuela | 859,575 | 3.8 |
| 7. People's Republic of China | 731,825 | 3.3 | 7. Nigeria | 841,325 | 3.7 |
| 8. Libya | 727,445 | 3.3 | 8. Kuwait | 808,475 | 3.5 |
| 9. Nigeria | 697,150 | 3.2 | 9. People's Republic of China | 773,800 | 3.4 |
| 10. Kuwait | 680,725 | 3.1 | 10. Libya | 753,725 | 3.3 |
| 11. United Arab Emirates | 668,680 | 3.0 | 11. United Arab Emirates | 669,775 | 2.9 |
| 12. Indonesia | 597,505 | 2.7 | 12. Indonesia | 580,350 | 2.5 |
| 13. Canada | 483,260 | 2.2 | 13. United Kingdom | 573,050 | 2.5 |
| 14. Algeria | 447,125 | 2.0 | 14. Canada | 545,675 | 2.4 |
| 15. Mexico | 440,555 | 2.0 | 15. Mexico[1] | 532,900 | 2.3 |
| 16. United Kingdom | 394,930 | 1.8 | 16. Algeria[1] | 414,275 | 1.8 |
| 17. Qatar | 176,537 | 0.8 | 17. Neutral Zone | 206,225 | 0.9 |
| 18. Neutral Zone | 170,090 | 0.8 | 18. Egypt | 186,150 | 0.8 |
| 19. Egypt | 169,360 | 0.8 | 19. Qatar | 184,325 | 0.8 |
| 20. Argentina | 165,195 | 0.8 | 20. Brunei-Malaysia | 182,500 | 0.8 |
| **Total World** | **22,158,251** | **100.0** | **Total World** | **22,765,050** | **100.0** |

(1) Includes lease condensate

### World Oil Supply and Demand Projections

(million barrels per day)
Source: Central Intelligence Agency

| | 1976 | 1977 | 1978 | 1979 | 1980 | 1985 |
|---|---|---|---|---|---|---|
| Demand (non-Communist) | 48.4 | 49.8-50.5 | 51.2-52.2 | 52.5-54.1 | 54.9-56.7 | 68.3-72.6 |
| United States | 16.7 | 17.8-18.3 | 18.2-19.0 | 18.4-19.7 | 19.3-20.7 | 22.2-25.6 |
| West Europe | 13.6 | 13.9-14.3 | 13.8-14.4 | 13.7-14.4 | 13.7-14.7 | 15.8-18.2 |
| Japan | 5.2 | 5.3-5.4 | 5.5-5.8 | 5.9-6.2 | 6.2-6.6 | 8.1-8.8 |
| Canada | 2.0 | 2.0-2.1 | 2.0-2.1 | 2.1-2.2 | 2.2-2.4 | 2.9-3.5 |
| Other developed[1] | 1.2 | 1.2 | 1.3 | 1.3 | 1.4 | 1.9 |
| Non-OPEC LDCs[2] | 6.7 | 7.1 | 7.1 | 7.5 | 8.5 | 12.0 |
| OPEC[3] countries | 2.1 | 2.3 | 2.5 | 2.8 | 3.0 | 4.0 |
| Other demand[4] | 0.9 | 0 | 0 | 0 | | |
| Non-OPEC supply[5] | 17.5 | 18.5 | 20.1 | 21.2 | 22.0 | 20.4-22.4 |
| United States | 9.7 | 9.6 | 10.2 | 10.2 | 10.0 | 4.0-11.0 |
| West Europe | 0.9 | 1.8 | 2.5 | 3.1 | 3.7 | 4.0-5.0 |
| Japan | 0 | | | | | 0.1 |
| Canada | 1.6 | 1.6 | 1.5 | 1.5 | 1.5 | 1.3-1.5 |
| Other developed[1] | 0.5 | 0.5 | 0.5 | 0.5 | 0.5 | 0.4 |
| Non-OPEC LDCs[2] | 3.7 | 4.1 | 4.6 | 5.3 | 6.1 | 8.0-9.0 |
| Net Communist trade[6] | 0.9 | 0.7 | 0.5 | 0.2 | − 0.3 | − 3.5—4.5 |
| USSR-East Europe | | | | | | |
| China | 0.2 | 0.2 | 0.3 | 0.4 | − 0.5 | 0 |
| Required OPEC production[7] | 30.9 | 31.3-32.0 | 31.1-32.1 | 31.3-32.9 | 32.9-34.7 | 46.7-51.2 |

(1) Australia, Israel, New Zealand, South Africa. (2) LDCs: less developed countries. (3) OPEC: Organization of Petroleum Exporting Countries. (4) Including stock changes and statistical discrepancy. (5) Including natural gas liquids. (6) Difference of Communist countries' exports and imports; minus sign indicates net Communist imports. (7) OPEC production capacity will reach 27.5-29.4 million barrels per day by 1985, exclusive of Saudi Arabia. Saudi projections are uncertain.

### U.S. Dependence on Petroleum Imports

Source: Department of Energy
(million barrels per day average)

| Source | 1974 | 1975 | 1976 | 1977 | 1978 | 1979 | 1980 (1st Qtr.) |
|---|---|---|---|---|---|---|---|
| Arab nations | 0.75 | 1.38 | 2.42 | 3.18 | 2.96 | 3.04 | 2.96 |
| All OPEC | 3.28 | 3.60 | 5.07 | 6.19 | 5.64 | 5.61 | 4.89 |
| All nations | 6.11 | 6.06 | 7.31 | 8.81 | 8.23 | 8.41 | 7.79 |
| U.S. production | 16.65 | 16.32 | 17.46 | 18.43 | 18.82 | 18.43 | 18.12 |

Fig. 59.  Footnote reference in almanac entry

for this page is (Sports—Track and Field Records; One-Mile Run; Table Tennis).

(Pole vaulting) is a (field event). By looking in the section (Field events), you find that (the record for the pole vault is 18 feet, 11 and one-half inches). This (pole vault record) was set by (a man from Poland on July 30, 1980, and the place the record was set was Moscow).

*OPTION 7: Asterisk used in entry*

In front of the (record number of feet jumped), there is an asterisk or star. The asterisk tells you that there is something you should know about this (record). To discover what an asterisk means, you must look either at the beginning or the end of the section. You will see another asterisk and an explanation of what it means here. I have copied the explanation for this asterisk at the bottom of this sample page. (*Pause*) In this case, it tells you that (the record given will probably be the new record, but it is not official yet).

Whenever you see an asterisk, you must look at the beginning or the end of the section to discover what it means. Using this same page of your booklet, can you discover (who holds the women's record for the one-mile run)? (*Pause*) Look under the section titled (Women's Records). (*Pause*) (The women's record holder for the one-mile-run is Mary Decker.) Is this (record official)? (*Pause*) There is an asterisk in front of (the record). Again it tells you that (this probably will be the record, but it is not yet official).

[End of Option 7]

Now, open (*The World Almanac*) on the table in front of you and turn to page (858). Page (858) is the same page you just looked at in your booklet. Turn to the beginning of this section on page (857). This is the page on which the (world track and field records) start. Notice that on the pages (before and after) page (858), there are other (sports records). (*Tone*) Did you find some interesting facts about (sports)? It is fun to read through this type of information in the almanac.

*OPTION 8: Footnote numbers in entries*

Turn back to your booklet and open it to page (13) (fig. 59). When you learned to use the index, one of the subjects you looked at was (the Organization of Petroleum Exporting Countries). (Two of) the pages given for (OPEC)

were (184 and 185). Page (13) of your booklet shows (pages 184 and 185). The information on (OPEC) is at (the bottom of page 184) under the topic (U.S. Petroleum Imports by Sources). (*Pause*)

Look at the (countries) listed under (Nation). After (Other OPEC), you will see a small numeral 1. (*Pause*) That small number is called a superior number. It tells the reader to look for more information. (*Pause*) To find what the superior number means, you must look at the bottom of the section (U.S. Petroleum Imports by Source). You should find the small numeral 1 followed by (the countries Ecuador, Gabon, Iraq, Kuwait, and Qatar). Those are the (countries that are included in Other OPEC countries).

Look at page (185) in your sample. Under the topic (World Oil Supply and Demand Projections), there is a section titled (Demand [non-Communist]). Under that you will see a list of (countries). What (countries) are listed as (Other developed)? (*Pause*) (Other developed) has a small numeral 1 after it. Can you find (what countries are part of Other developed)? (*Pause*) Did you look at the end of the section and find the little numeral 1? You should have discovered that (the countries listed as [Other developed] are Australia, Israel, New Zealand, and South Africa). Congratulations! You will soon be an expert at using the almanac.

[End of Option 8]

Sometimes when you look in the index, you may not find the subject you want even though that subject is in the almanac. When this happens, you must become a detective. Let's look at an example. If you want to know where (Olivia Newton-John) was born, you might look in the index under (her) last name. There isn't a listing for (Newton-John, Olivia), so you must try something else. You know that (Olivia Newton-John) is a (singer). Turn to page (14) (fig. 60) in your booklet. Page (14) shows a copy of the index entry (Singers, noted). The page(s) given in the index for (Singers, noted) are pages (369 to 383).

```
Singers, noted.................369-383
```

FIG. 60.   Where to look for information about a popular singer

Noted Personalities — Popular Songs; Entertainers

369

Noted Personalities—Entertainers

376

**Entertainment Personalities — Where and When Born**

Actors, Actresses, Dancers, Musicians, Producers, Radio-TV Performers, Singers

| Name | Birthplace | Born |
| --- | --- | --- |

Fig. 61.  Entertainers, when and where they were born

Copyright © 1980 by Newspaper Enterprise Association, Inc. Reprinted from *The World Almanac & Book of Facts 1981*, pp.369, 376, by permission of the publisher.

Go on to page (15) (fig. 61). A copy of page (369) is shown on the left hand side of page (15) of your booklet. (*Pause*) Page (369) has the heading, (Entertainment Personalities—Where and When Born). Under this heading, there is a list of the (types of entertainers) included. This section tells about (actors, actresses, dancers, musicians, producers, radio-TV performers, and singers). (Olivia Newton-John) is a (singer), so this is the section of the almanac to find out where (she) was born.

Look at the (names) listed on page (369). This list is in alphabetical order. You must find page (376) to actually locate (Olivia Newton-John). Page (376) is included among the pages shown in the index. The pages given in the index were (367 to 383). Page (376) is copied on the right-hand side of page (15) in your booklet. On page (376), can you find where (Olivia Newton-John) was born? (*Pause*) If you discovered that (Olivia Newton-John) was born in (Cambridge, England), you are becoming a great fact detective!

The almanac is especially helpful in finding who a government's leaders are. The people in these offices change from time to time, so it's hard to remember who holds the different offices. Try to use your copy of (*The World Almanac*) to discover who our governor is. You can begin by looking for the subject heading, Governors, or you can look for the name of our state (*name your state*). If you look for (*name your state*), look for the subheading, Governor. Now see if you can discover who the governor of (*name your state*) is. (*Tone*) If you discovered that (*name of governor*) is the governor of (*name your state*), you have learned how to use the almanac correctly.

Now take some time and use the almanac in front of you to look for things that interest you. There are so many interesting facts in the almanac that you could spend hours looking at it. Remember, you can play the tape again and review the pages of your booklet if you wish. When you feel confident that you know how to find information in the almanac, you may get the worksheet from (*your name*).

## WORKSHEET

1.   Use the index to find the page numbers for the following subjects:

   a.   Grand Canyon _____

   b.   Public School Enrollment _____

   c.   Movie Stars _____

   d.   Boston Marathon _____

2.   Find the answers to the following questions by using your copy of
     the almanac:

   a.   Who was the 14th President of the United States? _____

        _____

   b.   Who was the first woman in space? _____

   c.   Who are the United States Senators from (your state)?

        _____

        _____

   d.   What is the tallest building in (your city or a large city

        near you)? _____

   e.   What is the population of (your) county? _____

   f.   How much rain does (name a large city in your state) usually

        get during January? _____

# 8 ATLASES

Map reading is a skill which will be utilized by students throughout their lives, since it is a reference skill with practical implications in our mobile society. Map reading has important functions beyond its use as the basic road map, however. In this kit, the student is introduced to some statistical concepts represented in map form in an atlas.

The student will learn to visualize map representations; recognize directional symbols; interpret scales, symbols, and legends; read gazetteer entries; and define lines of longitude and latitude. The student will also read population, elevation, industrial, and natural resource maps.

## Materials Needed:

1 Atlas (Sample used: *Hammond World Atlas for Students: New Revised Edition*, 1980) Size 8½″ x 11″ preferred
6 Colored pencils (red, blue, green, yellow, orange, and brown)
1 Felt-tip pen (black)
1 Two- or three-ring notebook binder
1 Blank cassette tape
1 Mimeo or ditto master.

## Preparing the Visual Book:

1. Use a copy machine to transfer the following atlas pages:
   a. Index page (*see* fig. 67).
   b. Map of North America—make 3 copies (*see* figs. 62, 63, 64, and 66).
   c. Map of the United States (*see* fig. 68).
2. From one copy of North American map, cut out the map directional orientation symbol (*see* fig. 63).
   a. Mount on 8½″ x 11″ sheet of paper.
   b. Label North, East, South, West.
3. From same map of North America, cut out legend (*see* fig. 64).
   a. Mount on 8½″ x 11″ sheet of paper.
   b. Color legend heading red.
   c. Circle scale of miles and/or kilometers.
   d. Color other legend information one color per item.
4. Mount other atlas reproductions on 8½″ x 11″ sheets of paper (optional).
5. Map of North America (*see* fig. 62):
   a. Draw a red line around outline of North America.
   b. Draw a heavy black line around your state and color it green (Option 1A).
   c. Draw a line to your state and label it (Option 1B).

6. Map of North America (*see* fig. 66):
    a. Draw a red circle around the directional symbol.
    b. Draw a blue line from Los Angeles, California, to Denver, Colorado.
    c. Draw a red line from Kansas City, Kansas, to Cleveland, Ohio.
    d. Draw a brown circle around the star showing Washington, D.C.
    e. Draw a green circle around the star showing Ottowa, Canada.
7. Index page (*see* fig. 67):
    a. Color the column heading and corresponding information
        1) Country—blue
        2) Area in square miles—red
        3) Area in square kilometers—yellow
        4) Population—brown
        5) Capital—green
        6) Plate number or page—orange.
    b. Draw a black box around the index reference numbers.
8. Map of United States (*see* fig. 68):
    a. Draw lines of longitude around state of Colorado.
    b. Draw lines of latitude around state of Colorado.
    c. Circle reference letters in black.
    d. Circle reference numbers in red.
9. Make a sample mileage scale (*see* fig. 65):
    a. Scale should be 3 inches long with ½ inch equalling 50 miles
    b. Draw 4 sample lines (A to B)
        1) 1½ inches
        2) 2½ inches
        3) 5 inches
        4) 1¼ inches.
10. Laminate the pages or insert into plastic protective sheaths for durability.
11. Punch two or three holes in each page.
12. Put illustrations (figs. 62–68) into notebook in sequence indicated by numerical order.

# Preparing the Script:

1. Read the script and select and/or substitute the terminology congruent with that used in your library/media center.

2. Choose Option 1A or 1B.
3. Select appropriate legend information to correspond to your legend.
4. If using samples other than those illustrated, make changes where necessary in the script.
5. Proofread the script to correct any oversights or errors.
6. Record the script onto the blank cassette tape.

# Preparing the Worksheet:

1. Type the worksheet as it is written if you are using *Hammond's World Atlas for Students*
    or
2. Substitute similar questions from the atlas you are using.

# Preparing for Student Use:

1. Arrange a table and chair.
2. Insert the recorded tape cassette into a cassette player with earphones.
3. Place a copy of the almanac used in the illustrations on the table.
4. Provide a ruler on the table.
5. Give the student the visual book.

# Script

Today, you are going to learn to use an atlas. You know that people use maps to find how to get to places when they don't know the way. Maps also have many other uses.

An atlas is a whole book of maps. The maps in an atlas can show you how far it is from one place to another. They can also help you find other

FIG. 62. Map of North America

Copyright © 1980 by C. S. Hammond & Co. Reprinted from *Hammond World Atlas for Students*, p.4, by permission of the publisher.

facts and information, as you will see today. The atlases in our (library/media center) can be found (*describe the location*). They (can/cannot) be checked out of the (library/media center).

You have a copy of the (*Hammond World Atlas for Students*) in front of you. This is the atlas you will be using today. Open your booklet to page 1 (fig. 62). (*Pause*) Page 1 is a map of North America. This map shows the outline of the North American continent as it would look if you were an astronaut looking down at the earth from outer space. I have drawn a red line around the edges of the continent to help you see how it looks. At the bottom of the page, you can see how the continent of South America joins the continent of North America.

The heavy lines inside the map of North America show how the states of the United States and the provinces of Canada are divided. You could not tell where states and provinces or countries begin and end if you were looking down from space. You could only see the continents. The continents show up because they are surrounded by water.

Lines are drawn for each state in this atlas to show you where each state is and where it is located in the United States.

*OPTION 1A: Large states*

I have drawn the line around (*name of your state*) darker and have colored it green.

*OPTION 1B: Small states*

Our state of (*name of your state*) is fairly small in size when it is shown on a map of North America like this one. Even though (*name of your state*) seems big to those of us who live here, it is not very big compared to the entire continent of North America. To help you find (*name of your state*), I have written (*name of your state*) in the area shown as the Atlantic Ocean and I have drawn a line to the place on the map where (*name of your state*) is located.

[End of Option 1]

(*Name of your state*) is located (*describe whether east or west, north or south and other distinctive descriptions that apply*).

Turn to page 2 (fig. 63) in your booklet. (*Pause*) On page 2, you will see a symbol that shows you which direction is North. You will find a similar symbol on every map showing places. The N for North should always be facing

you as it is on page 2. You may have to turn the atlas around until the N is facing the right way.

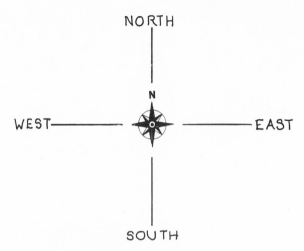

FIG. 63.    Direction symbol

Copyright © 1980 by C. S. Hammond & Co. Reprinted from *Hammond World Atlas for Students*, p.4, by permission of the publisher.

Look at page 3 (fig. 64) in your booklet. (*Pause*) Page 3 shows you a legend for the map of North America that you looked at on page 1. A legend tells you what symbols are used on the map. At the top of the legend, and colored red on your page, is the name of the map. This legend is for a map of North America.

Next, in the space circled in black, are two scales. The first is labeled ("Scale of Miles"), and the second, ("Scale of Kilometers"). The scale is to help you figure out how far apart places are. By using your ruler and the scale you can discover how many miles it is from one place to another. You will learn how to use a scale in just a minute. First, let's look at the rest of the legend.

Capitals of countries, on this map, are marked

FIG. 64.    Legend for the map of North America

Copyright © 1980 by C. S. Hammond & Co. Reprinted from *Hammond World Atlas for Students*, p.4, by permission of the publisher.

with (a star). I have colored this legend information green on your sample. Because this is a map of North America, there will be several capitals of countries on the map.

Next, colored yellow, is the symbol for international boundaries. International boundaries are imaginary lines that divide countries. (A heavy line followed by two dots) shows the borders of each country. A line like this will show where the United States and Canada meet.

The next symbol, colored blue, shows (other boundaries). (Other boundaries) show how (states) are marked on the map.

The (last) symbol on this legend, colored orange, shows the symbol for (canals). An example of (a canal) would be (the Panama Canal that connects the Atlantic and Pacific Oceans. It is located in the country of Panama). (*List any other symbols on your legend and explain what each means.*)

Now go on to page 4 (fig. 65). This page will help you learn to use a scale. At the top of the page is a scale of miles as it might look on a legend. Use your ruler and measure from zero to fifty. Put the end of your ruler on zero. From zero to fifty miles is one-half inch. How many inches show 100 miles? (*Pause*) On this scale, 100 miles are shown by one inch. How many miles are shown by two inches on your ruler? (*Pause*) Two inches on a map using this scale indicate a distance of 200 miles.

Now, let's try some of the samples on page 4. Look at sample number 1. How far apart are A and B? (*Pause*) Did you measure one and one-half inches? (*Pause*) Now move your ruler up to the scale of miles. (*Pause*) Put the end of your ruler on the zero and measure one and one-half inches. According to the scale, these two places would be 150 miles apart.

Try sample 2 by yourself. Measure the line from A to B, then use the scale of miles to see how many miles apart the two places would be. (*Tone*) Did you find that A and B were two and one-half inches apart? Using the scale of miles, did you find that it is 250 miles from A to B? If you did this correctly, you are ready to go on to sample 3. If you didn't get the right answer, stop the tape and try again. (*Pause*)

You are doing so well, you are now ready for sample 3. Look at how far the distance is from A to B. The scale is not that long. Can you figure out what to do? Try it and then we will go over the steps together. See if you can figure out how far it is from A to B in sample number 3. (*Tone*)

With your ruler, measure from A to B. It is five inches from A to B. How many miles are there in one inch? (*Pause*) Yes, one inch equals 100 miles. How many miles are shown by two inches? (*Pause*) Two inches are 200 miles. Three inches are 300 miles, so four inches would be how many miles? (*Pause*) Yes, 400 miles. Now, how many miles are shown by five inches? (*Pause*) Great! On the map using this scale, five inches are equal to 500 miles.

Let's go on to sample 4. This sample is how long on your ruler? (*Pause*) Measuring from A to B, you find that A and B are one and one-quarter inches apart. Now, use your scale of miles and see if you can figure out how many miles A is from B. (*Tone*) From A to B is a distance of about 125 miles. Maps, such as these, are not made to tell you that it is 132 miles from A to B. The legend only helps to give you an idea of about how many miles it is from one place to another.

You are ready for page 5 (fig. 66) of your booklet. This is the same map of North America that you looked at before.

Notice the N pointing to the direction North. I have drawn a red circle around it to help you find it on the page. Look in the lower left-hand corner. This is the legend that you looked at before. What does this legend tell us about this map? (*Pause*) Yes, the legend tells us that this is a map of North America. Look at the scale of miles. 100 miles shown on this scale is smaller than 100 miles on the sample scale you used. A map of North America in an atlas must be made so small that places 100 miles apart look close together.

I have drawn a blue line from Los Angeles, California, to Denver, Colorado. Using your ruler and the scale of miles in the legend, can you find about how many miles it is from Los Angeles to Denver? (*Tone*) It is approximately one and one-half inches from Los Angeles to Denver on this map. Using the scale, we can see that it is approximately 800 miles from Los Angeles to Denver. Of course, this would be the number of miles in a straight line. If you were driving, it probably would be a little longer, because highways do not go in a straight line.

Let's try one more. I have drawn a red line from Kansas City, Kansas, to Cleveland, Ohio. Find out about how many miles it is from Kansas City to Cleveland. (*Tone*) It is approximately 700 miles from Kansas City to Cleveland.

The legend told you that (capitals of countries) are marked with (a star). The capital of the

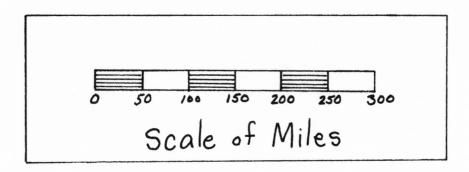

Scale of Miles

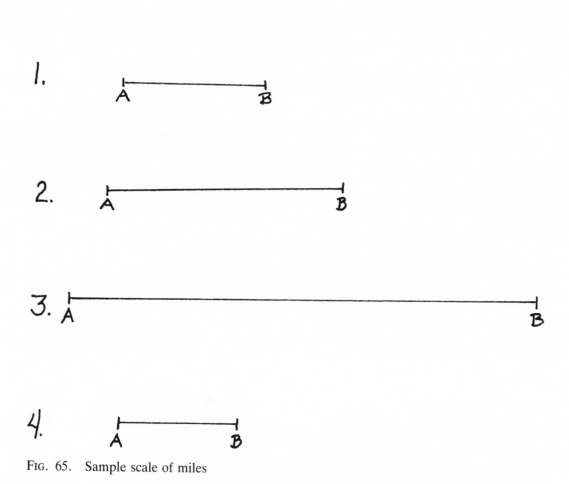

FIG. 65.    Sample scale of miles

United States is Washington, D.C. It is difficult to find the (star) for Washington, D.C., on this map, so I have drawn a brown circle around it to help you. (*Pause*) The capital of Canada is Ottawa. I have drawn a green circle around Ottawa to help you find it. (*Pause*) Now, see if you can find the capital of Mexico. Mexico is below or south of the United States. What is the capital of Mexico? (*Tone*) Did you find the (star) that shows that Mexico City is the capital of Mexico? (*Pause*) If you didn't find it, stop the tape until you do. (*Pause*) Now, compare this page of your booklet with the map on page (4) of your atlas. Take as much time as you need to look at page (4). (*Tone*) Because an atlas is a book of many maps, you need an index to help you find the map you want without searching through the entire atlas.

Fig. 66. Determining distances on map of
North America

Copyright © 1980 by C. S. Hammond & Co. Reprinted from *Hammond World Atlas for Students*, p.4, by permission of the publisher.

Page 6 (fig. 67) in your booklet is a copy of one page of the (*Hammond World Atlas for Students*) index. The page has the heading (World Atlas and Gazetteer: Gazetteer–Index). (The word "gazetteer" means that this page will give you a few brief facts about each index entry.)

Let's look at the index entry for (Colorado—*if you live in Colorado, choose another state*). The name (Colorado, U.S.A.), is colored blue in your booklet. The heading at the top of the column is also colored blue. In this index entry you learn that the state of (Colorado) is part of the United States of America. Next, colored red at the heading and in the second column of this index entry, you see the figure that tells you the number of square miles in the state of (Colorado). (Colorado) covers (104,247) square miles. The heading and the information in the third column are colored yellow. This column tells you the number of square kilometers in the state of (Colorado). There are (270,000) square kilometers of land in (Colorado). The fourth column gives you information about population in (Colorado). The heading at the top of the column is colored brown. So is the figure that tells you there were (2,207,259) people living in (Colorado) when the people in that state were counted in the last census.

In the next column, colored green, is the capital of (Colorado). The capital of (Colorado) is (Denver). Look at the column head and the number colored orange. This gives you the (plate number or) page number. By turning to the map on page (8) in the atlas, you will find a map that shows (Colorado).

The numbers inside the black box are the index reference numbers. The index reference numbers for (Colorado) are (G-5). Turn to page 7 (fig. 68) in your booklet and you will see how these index reference numbers can help you. (*Pause*) Page 7 in your booklet is a copy of the map found on page (8) in the atlas. At the top and bottom of this page are letters of the alphabet. I have circled these in black. The letters at the top are: (A, B, C, D, E, F, G, H, J). (The letter "I" is left out because it looks too much like a "J.") At the bottom of the page, you see the letters: (D, E, F, G, H, J). The index reference letter for (Colorado) was (G). Find (G) at the top and the bottom of the page. (*Pause*) On either side of the (G) are lines. I have drawn these lines in black on either side of the (G).

Notice that the spaces between the lines get wider at the bottom. A map is drawn on a flat piece of paper, but it shows a picture of part of the world and the world is round. These imaginary lines on the map go from the North Pole to the Equator and are called lines of longitude. So that the map can show the earth as it really is, these lines of longitude must spread out as they go from pole to equator.

Now, look along the (left/right) side of the page. There are some numbers. The numbers along the side of the page are (1, 2, 3, 4, 5, 6, 7, 8, 9). (Page [8] in the atlas is part of a map that covers two pages so there are no numbers on the [left-/right-] hand side.) I have circled these numbers with red. Notice that again there are lines on either side of the numbers. These lines curve across the page and are called lines of latitude. Lines of latitude are imaginary lines that go around the world. The equator is a line of latitude.

The lines of latitude on either side of the index reference number (5) have been colored red on the map to help you see how they curve across the page.

Now, find where the black lines of longitude for (G) and the red lines of latitude for (5) join to form a shape that is almost a square. Inside of this shape you will find the state of (Colorado). The state actually goes a little beyond these lines, but by using the index reference numbers, you can quickly find it.

Now, pick up your copy of the (*Hammond World Atlas for Students*) and turn to the index page. It is in the (front/back) of your atlas and is labeled (World Atlas and Gazetteer: Gazetteer-Index). (*Tone*) Use the index to find the entry for (*name of your state*). (Remember, the index is on more than one page.) (*Tone*) You have found the index entry for (*name of your state*). Let's see if you can find the answers to some questions about our state. What is the capital of (*name of your state*)? (*Pause*) Our capital is (*name*). How big is our state in miles? (*Pause*) (*Name of your state*) covers (*specify*) square miles. What is the population of (*name of your state*)? (*Pause*) Did you discover that (*name of your state*) has (*specify*) number of people?

What page (or plate number) will you turn to for a map of (*name of your state*)? (*Pause*) Did you say page (*specify*)? Great! What are the index reference numbers for (*name of your state*)? (*Pause*) Yes, the index reference numbers are (*specify*). Now, turn to page (*specify*) in the atlas and use your index reference numbers

# WORLD ATLAS AND GAZETTEER

## GAZETTEER-INDEX

This alphabetical list of grand divisions, countries, states, colonial possessions, etc., gives area, population, capital or chief town, and index references and page numbers on which they are shown on the largest scale. The index reference shows the square on the respective map in which the name of the entry may be located.

| (Color blue) Country | (Color red) Area (Sq. Miles) | (Color yellow) Area (Sq. Km) | (Color brown) Population | (Color green) Capital or Chief Town | (Color orange) Index Ref. | Plate No. |
|---|---|---|---|---|---|---|
| *Afghanistan | 250,000 | 647 500 | 17,078,263 | Kabul | B 2 | 34 |
| Africa | 11,682,000 | 30 256 380 | 345,000,000 | | | 46 |
| Alabama, U.S.A. | 51,609 | 133 667 | 3,444,165 | Montgomery | M 6 | 9 |
| Alaska, U.S.A. | 586,412 | 1 518 807 | 302,173 | Juneau | F 8 | 8 |
| *Albania | 11,100 | 28 749 | 2,126,000 | Tiranë | G 4 | 20 |
| Alberta, Canada | 255,285 | 661 188 | 1,627,874 | Edmonton | E 5 | 5 |
| *Algeria | 919,595 | 2 381 751 | 13,547,000 | Algiers | G 4 | 46 |
| American Samoa | 76 | 197 | 27,159 | Pago Pago | J 7 | 44 |
| Andorra | 175 | 453 | 19,000 | Andorra la Vella | G 1 | 27 |
| *Angola | 481,351 | 1 246 699 | 5,430,000 | Luanda | J13 | 47 |
| Antarctica | 5,500,000 | 14 245 000 | | | | 48 |
| Antigua & Dep. | 171 | 443 | 63,000 | St. John's | G 3 | 14 |
| *Argentina | 1,072,070 | 2 776 661 | 23,983,000 | Buenos Aires | H10 | 19 |
| Arizona, U.S.A. | 113,909 | 295 024 | 1,772,482 | Phoenix | E 6 | 8 |
| Arkansas, U.S.A. | 53,104 | 137 539 | 1,923,295 | Little Rock | K 6 | 9 |
| Ascension | 34 | 88 | 1,486 | Georgetown | D13 | 47 |
| Asia | 17,032,000 | 44 112 880 | 2,043,997,000 | | | 31 |
| *Australia | 2,967,741 | 7 686 449 | 12,630,000 | Canberra | | 42 |
| *Austria | 32,374 | 83 849 | 7,419,341 | Vienna | F 4 | 20 |
| *Bahamas | 5,382 | 13 939 | 197,000 | Nassau | C 1 | 14 |
| *Bahrain | 231 | 598 | 207,000 | Manama | E 4 | 32 |
| *Bangladesh | 55,126 | 142 776 | 70,000,000 | Dacca | F 4 | 34 |
| *Barbados | 166 | 430 | 253,620 | Bridgetown | G 4 | 14 |
| *Belgium | 11,779 | 30 508 | 9,660,154 | Brussels | E 3 | 20 |
| Belize | 8,867 | 22 965 | 122,000 | Belmopan | C 2 | 12 |
| *Benin | 43,483 | 112 621 | 3,029,000 | Porto-Novo | G10 | 46 |
| Bermuda | 21 | 54 | 52,000 | Hamilton | G 2 | 14 |
| *Bhutan | 18,000 | 46 620 | 770,000 | Thimphu | G 3 | 34 |
| *Bolivia | 424,163 | 1 098 582 | 4,804,000 | La Paz, Sucre | G 7 | 18 |
| *Botswana | 219,815 | 569 321 | 629,000 | Gaborone | M16 | 47 |
| *Brazil | 3,284,426 | 8 506 663 | 90,840,000 | Brasília | K 6 | 18 |
| British Columbia, Canada | 366,255 | 948 600 | 2,184,621 | Victoria | D 5 | 5 |
| British Indian Ocean Territory | 23 | 60 | 600 | London (U.K.) | L10 | 31 |
| Brunei | 2,226 | 5 765 | 130,000 | Bandar Seri Begawan | E 4 | 38 |
| *Bulgaria | 42,829 | 110 927 | 8,501,000 | Sofia | G 4 | 20 |
| *Burma | 261,789 | 678 033 | 27,000,000 | Rangoon | C 3 | 40 |
| *Burundi | 10,747 | 27 835 | 3,475,000 | Bujumbura | M12 | 47 |
| California, U.S.A. | 158,693 | 411 015 | 19,953,134 | Sacramento | C 5 | 8 |
| *Cambodia | 69,898 | 181 036 | 6,701,000 | Phnom Penh | E 5 | 40 |
| *Cameroon | 183,568 | 475 441 | 5,836,000 | Yaoundé | J10 | 46 |
| *Canada | 3,851,809 | 9 976 185 | 21,568,311 | Ottawa | | 5 |
| *Cape Verde | 1,557 | 4 033 | 285,000 | Praia | H 5 | 3 |
| Cayman Islands | 100 | 259 | 10,652 | Georgetown | B 3 | 14 |
| *Central African Republic | 240,534 | 622 983 | 1,518,000 | Bangui | K11 | 46 |
| Central America | 196,928 | 510 043 | 16,090,000 | | | 12 |
| *Ceylon (Sri Lanka) | 25,332 | 65 610 | 12,300,000 | Colombo | D 7 | 34 |
| (Color yellow) *Chad | 495,752 | 1 283 998 | 3,869,000 | N'Djamena | K 9 | 46 |
| Channel Islands | 75 | 194 | 117,000 | St. Helier | E 6 | 22 (Color brown) |
| (Color red) Chile | 292,257 | 756 946 | 8,834,820 | Santiago | F10 | 19 |
| *China (People's Republic) | 3,691,506 | 9 561 000 | 740,000,000 | Peking | | 36 (Color green) |
| China (Taiwan) | 13,948 | 36 125 | 14,577,000 | Taipei | K 7 | 36 |
| (Color blue) Colombia | 439,513 | 1 138 339 | 21,117,000 | Bogotá | E 3 | 18 |
| Colorado, U.S.A. | 104,247 | 270,000 | 2,207,259 | Denver | G 5 | 8 (Color orange) |
| Comoros | 719 | 1 862 | 266,000 | Moroni | P14 | 47 |
| *Congo | 132,046 | 341 999 | 915,000 | Brazzaville | J12 | 47 |
| Connecticut, U.S.A. | 5,009 | 12 973 | 3,032,217 | Hartford | O 2 | 9 |
| Cook Islands | 93 | 241 | 20,000 | Avarua | L 8 | 44 |
| *Costa Rica | 19,575 | 50 699 | 1,800,000 | San José | E 5 | 12 |
| *Cuba | 44,206 | 114 493 | 8,553,395 | Havana | B 2 | 14 |
| *Cyprus | 3,473 | 8 995 | 649,000 | Nicosia | B 2 | 32 |
| *Czechoslovakia | 49,370 | 127 868 | 14,497,000 | Prague | F 4 | 20 |
| Delaware, U.S.A. | 2,057 | 5 328 | 548,104 | Dover | P 5 | 9 |
| *Denmark | 16,625 | 43 059 | 4,910,000 | Copenhagen | E 9 | 25 |
| District of Columbia, U.S.A. | 67 | 173 | 756,510 | Washington | O 5 | 9 |
| *Djibouti | 8,880 | 22 999 | 250,000 | Djibouti | P 9 | 46 |
| Dominica | 290 | 751 | 70,302 | Roseau | G 4 | 14 |
| *Dominican Rep. | 18,704 | 48 443 | 4,011,589 | Santo Domingo | D 3 | 14 |
| *Ecuador | 109,483 | 283 561 | 6,144,000 | Quito | E 4 | 18 |
| *Egypt | 386,100 | 999 999 | 35,900,000 | Cairo | N 5 | 46 |
| *El Salvador | 8,260 | 21 393 | 3,418,455 | San Salvador | C 4 | 12 |
| England, U.K. | 50,327 | 130 347 | 46,102,300 | London | F 4 | 22 |
| *Equatorial Guinea | 10,831 | 28 052 | 305,100 | Malabo | G11 | 46 |

| Country | Area (Sq. Miles) | Area (Sq. Km) | Population | Capital or Chief Town | Index Ref. | Plate No. |
|---|---|---|---|---|---|---|
| *Ethiopia | 471,776 | 1 221 900 | 24,764,000 | Addis Ababa | O10 | 46 |
| Europe | 4,063,000 | 10 523 170 | 644,574,000 | | | 20 |
| Faerøe Is., Den. | 540 | 1 399 | 38,000 | Tórshavn | D 2 | 20 |
| Falkland Is. | 4,618 | 11 961 | 2,000 | Stanley | H14 | 19 |
| *Fiji | 7,015 | 18 169 | 519,000 | Suva | H 8 | 44 |
| *Finland | 130,128 | 337 031 | 4,706,000 | Helsinki | | 25 |
| Florida, U.S.A. | 58,560 | 151 670 | 6,789,443 | Tallahassee | M 7 | 9 |
| *France | 212,841 | 551 258 | 50,770,000 | Paris | | 23 |
| French Guiana | 35,135 | 91 000 | 48,000 | Cayenne | K 3 | 18 |
| French Polynesia | 1,544 | 3 999 | 109,000 | Papeete | M 7 | 44 |
| *Gabon | 103,346 | 267 666 | 500,000 | Libreville | H11 | 47 |
| *Gambia | 4,003 | 10 368 | 357,000 | Banjul | C 9 | 46 |
| Georgia, U.S.A. | 58,876 | 152 489 | 4,589,575 | Atlanta | N 6 | 9 |
| *Germany, East (German Democratic Rep.) | 41,814 | 108 298 | 17,117,000 | Berlin | | 24 |
| *Germany, West (Federal Rep.) | 95,959 | 248 534 | 61,194,600 | Bonn | | 24 |
| *Ghana | 91,843 | 237 873 | 8,545,561 | Accra | G10 | 46 |
| Gibraltar | 2 | 5 | 27,000 | Gibraltar | D 4 | 27 |
| *Great Britain and Northern Ireland (United Kingdom) | 94,214 | 244 014 | 55,534,000 | London | | 22 |
| *Greece | 50,548 | 130 919 | 8,838,000 | Athens | G 5 | 20 |
| Greenland (Kalâtdlit-Nunât) | 840,000 | 2 175 600 | 47,000 | Godthåb (Nûk) | O 3 | 4 |
| *Grenada | 133 | 344 | 96,000 | St. George's | G 4 | 14 |
| Guadeloupe and Dep. | 687 | 1 779 | 324,000 | Basse-Terre | F 3 | 14 |
| Guam | 209 | 541 | 84,996 | Agaña | | 44 |
| *Guatemala | 42,042 | 108 889 | 5,200,000 | Guatemala | B 3 | 12 |
| *Guinea | 94,925 | 245 856 | 3,890,000 | Conakry | D10 | 46 |
| *Guinea-Bissau | 13,948 | 36 125 | 517,000 | Bissau | C 9 | 46 |
| *Guyana | 83,000 | 214 970 | 763,000 | Georgetown | J 2 | 18 |
| *Haiti | 10,694 | 27 697 | 4,867,190 | Port-au-Prince | D 3 | 14 |
| Hawaii, U.S.A. | 6,450 | 16 705 | 769,913 | Honolulu | H 8 | 8 |
| *Holland (Netherlands) | 13,958 | 36 151 | 13,077,000 | Amsterdam, The Hague | E 3 | 20 |
| *Honduras | 43,277 | 112 087 | 2,495,000 | Tegucigalpa | D 3 | 12 |
| Hong Kong | 398 | 1 031 | 4,089,000 | Victoria | H 7 | 36 |
| *Hungary | 35,915 | 93 020 | 10,315,597 | Budapest | F 4 | 20 |
| *Iceland | 39,768 | 102 999 | 203,000 | Reykjavík | C 2 | 20 |
| Idaho, U.S.A. | 83,557 | 216 413 | 713,008 | Boise | E 3 | 8 |
| Illinois, U.S.A. | 56,400 | 146 076 | 11,113,976 | Springfield | L 4 | 9 |
| *India | 1,269,339 | 3 287 588 | 586,266,000 | New Delhi | | 34 |
| Indiana, U.S.A. | 36,291 | 93,994 | 5,193,669 | Indianapolis | M 5 | 9 |
| *Indonesia | 788,430 | 2 042 034 | 131,255,000 | Djakarta | | 38 |
| Iowa, U.S.A. | 56,290 | 145 791 | 2,825,041 | Des Moines | K 4 | 9 |
| *Iran | 636,293 | 1 647 999 | 28,448,000 | Tehran | F 2 | 32 |
| *Iraq | 167,924 | 434 923 | 9,431,000 | Baghdad | D 3 | 32 |
| *Ireland | 26,600 | 68 894 | 2,944,000 | Dublin | C 4 | 22 |
| Isle of Man, U.K. | 227 | 588 | 50,000 | Douglas | D 3 | 22 |
| *Israel | 7,993 | 20 702 | 2,911,000 | Jerusalem | C 3 | 32 |
| *Italy | 116,303 | 301 225 | 54,504,000 | Rome | | 26 |
| *Ivory Coast | 124,503 | 322 463 | 4,800,000 | Abidjan | E10 | 46 |
| *Jamaica | 4,411 | 11 424 | 1,972,000 | Kingston | C 3 | 14 |
| (Color orange) *Japan | 143,622 | 371 981 | 103,613,000 | Tokyo | N 4 | 36 |
| *Jordan | 37,297 | 96 599 | 2,300,000 | Amman | C 3 | 32 |
| Kalâtdlit-Nunât (Greenland) | 840,000 | 2 175 600 | 47,000 | Nûk (Godthåb) | O 3 | 4 |
| Kansas, U.S.A. | 82,264 | 213 064 | 2,249,071 | Topeka | J 5 | 8 |
| Kentucky, U.S.A. | 40,395 | 104 623 | 3,219,311 | Frankfort | M 5 | 9 |
| *Kenya | 224,960 | 582 646 | 10,880,200 | Nairobi | O12 | 47 |
| *Kiribati (land) | 290 | 751 | 47,922 | Bairiki | H 5 | 44 |
| Korea, North | 46,540 | 120 539 | 13,300,000 | P'yŏngyang | L 4 | 36 |
| Korea, South | 38,452 | 99 591 | 31,683,000 | Seoul | L 4 | 36 |
| *Kuwait | 6,532 | 16 918 | 1,100,000 | Al Kuwait | E 4 | 32 |
| *Laos | 91,459 | 236 879 | 2,900,000 | Vientiane | D 2 | 40 |
| *Lebanon | 4,015 | 10 399 | 2,800,000 | Beirut | B 3 | 32 |
| *Lesotho | 11,716 | 30 344 | 930,000 | Maseru | M17 | 47 |
| *Liberia | 43,000 | 111 370 | 1,200,000 | Monrovia | D10 | 46 |
| *Libya | 679,359 | 1 759 540 | 1,900,000 | Tripoli | K 6 | 46 |
| Liechtenstein | 61 | 158 | 21,000 | Vaduz | F 4 | 20 |
| Louisiana, U.S.A. | 48,523 | 125 675 | 3,643,180 | Baton Rouge | L 7 | 9 |
| *Luxembourg | 999 | 2 587 | 339,000 | Luxembourg | E 4 | 20 |
| Macao | 6.2 | 16 | 292,000 | Macao | H 7 | 36 |
| *Madagascar | 226,657 | 587 042 | 7,011,563 | Antananarivo | R15 | 47 |

*Members of the United Nations

Fig. 67. Gazetteer–Index

(*specify*) to find (*name of your state*). If you have trouble finding it, check your numbers in the index. (*Tone*) Did you find (*name of your state*) on page (*specify*)? You are becoming a good map reader! You are ready to go on.

Maps that show places are just one kind of map. An atlas may have many kinds of maps. Let's look at the (cover/page [specify]) in your copy of (*Hammond World Atlas for Students*). This is a map that shows how many people live in different parts of the world. It is called a population map. The legend tells you that (each dot represents or stands for [750,000] people). Can you find North America? (*Pause*) Some parts of North America are heavily populated, which means that there are many people living near each other. Other parts of North America have very few people. These areas are sparsely populated. Where we live (there are many people/is not a crowded area of North America).

Turn to page (7) in your (*Hammond World Atlas for Students*). (*Pause*) The map (at the top of/on) page (7) shows high and low areas of land in the United States. The lowest areas are near sea level and they are colored (green). Where the land is higher above sea level, the (green is lighter). The mountain areas are (brown with lines to look like mountains).

(On the bottom of page [7]/turn to page [*specify*] [*Pause*]), you see another map of the United States. This map shows (how the land is used, where industries are located, and where different natural resources are found). Find (*name of your state*). (*Pause*) Remember, it is (*describe location and shape*).

(What are the major crops/what types of farms) do we have in (*name of your state*)? (*Pause*) Check the legend labeled (dominant land use). (*Pause*) (*Name of your state*) is known for (*specify*). Do we have any (industrial areas) in (*name of your state*)? (*Pause*) (*Name of your state*) (has [*specify the types of industry*]/does not have [*any major industry*].) What (minerals) are found in (*name of your state*)? (*Pause*) We have (*name the [minerals]*) in our state.

The maps we have talked about today are just a few of the types of maps that can be found in an atlas. Take some time now, after you stop the tape and rewind it, to look at some more maps in the atlas. When you feel you are ready for the worksheet, come and get it from (*your name*). Good luck!

[End of Script]

◄ FIG. 68.   Map of the western United States

## WORKSHEET

1.   What is the capital of Florida? _____

2.   What are the index reference numbers for the state of Maine?

     _____

3.   On page 9, what state has the index reference numbers, M6?

     _____

4.   On page 20, find the capital of Spain. _____

5.   How many square miles does Illinois cover? _____

6.   On page 42, find about how many miles it is from Melbourne to

     Sydney. _____

7.   On page 18, find the index reference numbers for Ecuador. _____

     _____

8.   On what page will you find a map of Oregon? _____

# 9 VERTICAL FILE

The vertical file is important because it is a repository of ephemeral materials, especially those items of local interest which may not appear in published sources of general interest. The subjects in your vertical file will be unique, but students will be able to apply their ability to use your vertical file to most vertical files found in school library media centers and public libraries.

The student, by study of this kit, will learn to recognize and distinguish the types of materials commonly found in a vertical file. The student will also discover when use of the vertical file will provide essential or supplemental resource material.

## Materials Needed:

1   Manila folder
1–2 Blank catalog cards (Option 1A)
    Sample vertical file materials (*see script*)
1   Felt-tip pen (black)
1   Blank cassette tape.

## Preparing the Sample File:

1. Collect samples of materials similar to those in your vertical file: newspaper clippings, periodical clippings, pamphlets, booklets, pictures, posters, maps (*see script*).
2. Mark each sample with a number or print numbers on paper, 2″ x 2″, and staple to samples.
3. Option 1A: type a sample "see" reference and/or a "see also" reference as found in your card catalog. Staple card(s) to front of sample folder.
4. Label file folder "Vertical File," in style used on your vertical file folders.

## Preparing the Script:

1. Read the script and select and/or substitute the terminology congruent with that used in your library/media center.
2. Select Option 1A, 1B, or 1C; Option 2A or 2B.
3. Choose script sections relating to samples you have selected.

4. Proofread script to correct any oversights or errors.
5. Record the script onto the blank cassette tape.

# Preparing for Student Use:

1. Place a table and chair close to your vertical file.
2. Insert the recorded tape cassette into a cassette player with earphones.
3. Give the student the sample file folder.

# Script

You are sitting in front of our vertical file. As you can see, the vertical file looks like (an ordinary file cabinet/*describe if you use boxes, etc.*). The vertical file is a treasure chest of materials that can be very helpful to you. Open the (top drawer) of the vertical file. (*Pause*) Each (drawer) has manila folders inside of it. Each folder is labeled with a subject heading. Inside of each folder you will find articles and materials about the subject marked on the outside.

Take a few minutes and look at the subject headings in the vertical file. Do not pull any folders out, just look at the subject headings in the vertical file. Remember, do not remove any folders. (*Tone*) Did you get an idea of the many different subjects included in our vertical file?

*OPTION 1A: Vertical file subjects indexed in the card catalog*
The subjects in our vertical file are cataloged in our card catalog. Only subject headings are cataloged. There are no catalog cards for authors or titles of materials found in the vertical file. Each card for a subject in the vertical file has the subject name and then ("see" and/or "see also") vertical file. There is a sample catalog card on the front of the folder I gave you. (*Pause*)

*OPTION 1B: Separate index for vertical file subjects*
The information in the vertical file is not cataloged in the card catalog. Instead, there is an index to tell you what subjects you will find in our vertical file. The index is located (*describe the location*). Take a few minutes and look at the index. (*Tone*)

*OPTION 1C: Vertical file subjects not cataloged or indexed*
Materials in the vertical file are not included in the card catalog. The card catalog has cards for materials that are permanent. Materials in the vertical file change from year to year, so I don't catalog them. When you use the vertical file, try to think of a subject heading for the information you want. For example, if you are looking for information about (German Shepherd puppies), you might look for the subjects, (Animals) or (Dogs). If you can't find a subject that has what you need, ask (*your name*) if there is anything on that subject in the vertical file.

[End of Option 1]

The materials located in the vertical file are put there because they would get lost on the regular shelves. If the vertical file materials were mixed in with the books (and audiovisual materials), you would not be able to find them. By putting these materials in folders, you can find them easily.

All of the folders in the vertical file are in alphabetical order by subject. Nothing is filed in the vertical file by author or title. Each folder may have a variety of materials in it, but everything in the folder will be about the subject marked on the folder.

We get materials for the vertical file from many places. I will talk to you about a few of the different kinds of materials you will find in the vertical file. Pick up the sample file I have given to you. The subject of the sample file is "vertical file." I have given this folder the subject heading "vertical file," because this folder will help you learn about the vertical file.

Newspaper clippings about a particular subject are placed in the vertical file. Open your folder and find a newspaper article. The newspaper article is marked with a number (1). (*Pause*) The newspaper clipping should be the first thing in your folder, but if it isn't, keep looking until you find it. (*Pause*) You should now be looking at a newspaper clipping with the title (*give the title of the clipping*).

When you learned to use the (*Children's Magazine Guide* and/or *Abridged Readers' Guide to Periodical Literature*), you discovered that some news is too current to be in books. Magazines are a good source of up-to-date information, but you can find the most current information in a newspaper.

We take the (*name the newspapers in your library/media center*) here at (*name of your school*). If we could save and index all of our newspapers, you could find articles on all events that have been reported in the paper. Unfortunately, we don't have room to store back issues of our papers. Even if we could save the papers, it would be impossible for me to make an index that would help you find what you need. Instead, I read the paper and cut out articles that I think may be of interest to some of the students in our school. I file these newspaper clippings in the vertical file for as long as there is interest on the subject.

Periodical clippings are another source of useful information. These are also placed in the vertical file. Find the clipping with the (2) marked on it. (*Pause*) At (*name of school*), we keep back issues of magazines indexed in (*Children's Magazine Guide* and/or the *Abridged Readers' Guide to Periodical Literature*) for (*number of years*) years. Sometimes there are excellent articles that will be useful longer than (*number of years*) years. I cut these articles out before we discard the magazines and put the articles in the vertical file. If I see a good article in a current magazine that I have at home, I cut it out and bring it for the vertical file.

Pamphlets too are kept in the vertical file. Find the pamphlet marked with the number (3). (*Pause*) The title of this pamphlet is (*give pamphlet title*). A pamphlet is an article that is printed as a single item. It is not part of a magazine or other publication. A pamphlet usually has only a few pages. The entire pamphlet will be about one subject.

We get pamphlets from many different places. Sometimes I send for a pamphlet through the mail and sometimes I pick up an interesting pamphlet right here in (*name of your city or town*). The United States government prints pamphlets on many subjects. Some government pamphlets are printed for people interested in very specialized subjects, but there are others that have useful information for students like you. These pamphlets are in the vertical file.

Now find the booklet marked number (4) (*Pause*) (*Title of booklet*) is the title of this booklet. A booklet is similar to a pamphlet, but it has more pages than a pamphlet. A booklet is a small paperback book that is too small to shelve with the books. Booklets, like pamphlets, have information on one single subject.

There is a picture in your folder marked with the number (5). (*Pause*) This is a picture of (*describe*). The pictures in the vertical file are small. (Our large pictures are located [*describe the location*]). The pictures in our vertical file include (magazine prints/photographs/picture post cards/small reprints/*tell about any type of picture included in your vertical file*). Pictures can help you understand something you have never seen. If you look at a picture of a skeleton, you can understand better what the bones in your body look like. It is often said, "a picture is worth a thousand words."

Look through the folder for the poster. It is marked number (6). (*Pause*) This is a poster of (*describe*). Sometimes I find a poster that I think will be helpful to someone. Because posters are difficult to shelve, I put them into the vertical file where they will be with other things on the same subject.

Next, find the map marked (7). (*Pause*) This is a map of (*describe*). Maps are very useful in helping you find places. You (have learned/will learn) how to read a map in the atlas unit. An atlas is a book of maps. Usually, it does not have detailed maps of small areas. State road maps (like the one you are looking at for [*name of your state*]) show the details of the state better than an atlas map.

There are many kinds of maps. Almost every place in the world has been mapped. There are even maps of the bottom of the ocean. There are also maps to help us find the stars, planets, and galaxies in the universe. There are maps for places that have never existed except in the pages of a book. You might find a map of (the land of Oz), for example. Some maps, such as maps of (our school/neighborhood/town/city), are of interest to only a few people. When I find a map like this, I add it to the vertical file. Other maps in our vertical file that may interest you are maps of (*describe any special maps in your vertical file*).

As you can see, the vertical file holds a lot of interesting information. Use it to add to the information you can find in books and magazines. The vertical file is special because it has (information on current news/items especially about our area/additional material on subjects in books and magazines).

*OPTION 2A: Vertical file materials checked out*
Materials in our vertical file can be checked out and taken to your classroom or home for you to use. To check out a folder from the vertical file (*describe the check-out procedure*).

*OPTION 2B: Vertical file materials not checked out*
Materials in our vertical file cannot be

checked out of the (library/media center). So that the materials will not get lost, the folders must be used here in the (library/media center). You may use folders from the vertical file whenever you are in the (library/media center).
[End of Option 2]

I have given you an idea of the great variety of materials that you can find in the vertical file. Take some more time to get acquainted with these materials—I think you will find that it is fun to look at the many interesting things in the vertical file. When you are ready to do the follow-up activity, come and see (your name).
[End of Script]

## FOLLOW-UP ACTIVITY

No worksheet has been prepared for this unit due to the diversity of materials found in vertical files. You may wish to do one of the following activities:

1.  Make a list of some materials that can be found in your vertical file and ask the student to find them.

2.  Write some questions that require the student to use the vertical file to find the answers.

# CONCLUSION

Now that you have read the chapters detailing each kit, you are ready to begin making the kits for your own library/media center. Select one kit to prepare first; the kit for parts of a book or the encyclopedia set are recommended for your first attempt.

Follow the directions given in the manual as you select the source material (book, encyclopedia set, etc.) and as you prepare the actual components according to the instructions detailed in the chapters of this manual. By proceeding methodically, step by step, you will soon have your first kit ready for student use.

Before setting the kit out for student use, try it yourself and check to see that the information is clear and factual as applied to your own library/media center. When you are satisfied with the kit, you are ready to introduce it to the students in your school.

You may invite student usage in several ways. A general announcement to an entire class will make students aware that this source is available for their use. At this time, you may want to demonstrate how the students are to use the kit independently.

You may wish to introduce the kit to students one at a time as the need arises. This method relies on student need and/or "word of mouth" publicity.

A third way to promote the use of the kit is by way of posters and signs announcing the new learning resource. This method can effectively create student interest.

After students have had a week or so of exposure to the kit, you may want to evaluate their assessment of the kit as a learning tool. This can be done informally by discussing the concept with students who have used the kit and students who have not used it.

There is no time frame for completing construction of the kits. Preparation of additional kits can continue as time permits. By adding the kits to the library/media center gradually, student interest is sustained and unnecessary preparation pressure is eliminated.

Remember that the kits are adaptable to the needs of your school. They are as flexible as you want to make them.

Designed by Vladimir Reichl

Composed by Modern Typographers, Inc.,
  in Linotron 202 Times Roman
  and Helvetica

Printed on 50-pound Warren's
  1854, a pH-neutral stock,
  and bound in 10-point
  Feedcote cover stock by
  the University of Chicago
  Printing Department

Pasá